SOCIAL TV

how marketers can
reach and engage audiences
by connecting television to
the web, social media, and mobile

MIKE PROULX
STACEY SHEPATIN

WILEY

John Wiley & Sons, Inc.

Published by John Wiley & Sons, Inc., Hoboken, New Jersey.
Published simultaneously in Canada.

For general information on our other products and services or for technical support, please contact our Customer Care Department within the United States at (800) 762-2974, outside the United States at (317) 572-3993 or fax (317) 572-4002.

Wiley publishes in a variety of print and electronic formats and by print-on-demand. Some material included with standard print versions of this book may not be included in e-books or in print-on-demand. If this book refers to media such as a CD or DVD that is not included in the version you purchased, you may download this material at http://booksupport.wiley.com. For more information about Wiley products, visit www.wiley.com.

ISBN: 978-1-118-16746-5 (cloth)

ISBN: 978-1-118-22633-9 (ebk)

ISBN: 978-1-118-23965-0 (ebk)

ISBN: 978-1-118-26423-2 (ebk)

Printed in the United States of America

10 9 8 7 6 5 4 3 2 1

For the late Don Harley.
Your mentorship has forever lighted my lamp.
—M.C.P.

For WJRD.
Keep watching!!!!
—S.S.H.

Contents

Preface

What Is in a Name?

Television has always been social. It would seem, then, that the name of our book, *Social TV*, implies that there is nothing new to say about the beloved entertainment medium. Yet that could not be further from the truth. Television nowadays is a very different experience than it was in 1941, when TV advertisements first began airing in the United States.[1]

According to its strictest definition, the phrase "social TV" was coined to depict the convergence of television and social media. However, social TV has often been used in recent years as a catchall expression when referring to the modern era of television. While we tend to prefer the former definition, we painted using broad brush strokes throughout the book.

Television's love affair with social media comprises a sizable chunk of our narrative. We also tackle the effect that mobile and tablet devices have had on the medium (Chapters 4 and 8) and examine the growing impact of Internet-connected TVs (Chapter 9). Recognizing that the blending of media also gives TV audiences a much more personalized experience, we even included a section dedicated to addressable advertising (Chapter 7).

We wrote this book as a guide for marketers. Each chapter illustrates a slice of the television landscape, fraught with examples and case studies, followed by a deep dive into the advertising implications that result. Mobile QR codes conclude each chapter. By simply scanning these with your smartphone, you will access "second screen" companion content that brings to life many of the examples we illustrate within the book.

We intend *Social TV* to appeal not only to brands but also agencies, television networks, content creators, educators, and even TV viewers. In order to keep the book manageable in size and scope, we focus primarily on broadcast television series and events. While we have included some content on news and sports, each of those verticals could be a book in and of themselves.

Though we interviewed nearly fifty companies and featured many additional ones throughout *Social TV*, it simply was not possible to include a description of or story about every player within the space. New companies with interesting solutions seem to crop up every week. So instead, we attempted to provide enough of a representative cross-section to help illustrate the most important trends that are impacting television today. You will also notice that—because things are changing at breakneck speed—Chapter 11 can only be accessed online. We purposefully waited to write the last chapter just as *Social TV* was released in order to bring you the most up-to-date information.

That is why one need not go back over seven decades to witness the profound shift in the media landscape. Television is changing before our very eyes. It is a perpetual work in progress; a living medium influenced by advances in technology and evolutions in human culture. Yet as TV continues to change in both form and function, it will forever remain social at its core. Welcome to *Social TV*.

—Mike and Stacey

Acknowledgments

Social TV is our first book and we did not know *exactly* what to expect throughout its 10-month proposal, development, and launch process. The two of us are both floored by the level of support we have received from our colleagues, friends, and families.

Our employer, Hill Holliday, has been rooting us on from the very beginning, and we want to give special thanks to Mike Sheehan, Karen Kaplan, Baba Shetty, Cindy Stockwell, and Adam Cahill. Additionally, there were several other people at the agency who contributed to the book's development. Thanks to Tracy Brady for her help with publicity. Scott Woolwine, Liz Colonto, and Mark Wong created the *Social TV* logo animation sequence. Thomas Peri is the photographer behind our cover headshots. Erica Sperry and Michael Abbott assisted with network buying research. Lenora Cushing advised us on business affairs. And Austin Gardner Smith designed the custom Tumblr theme for the book's companion website.

We also want to thank the team at Wiley (Dan Ambrosio, Christine Moore, and Kim Dayman) for guiding us along the way.

Our book would be nothing without its content and we want to thank the people who provided us excellent seed material from which to write. In total, we spoke with nearly 50 different companies and over 75 industry leaders in order to glean background content, case studies, and/or direct quotes. Each of the following people enthusiastically made themselves available for meetings or conference calls and, in many cases, multiple follow-ups:

- ABC: Geri Wang, Rick Mandler, and Andrew Messina
- Backchannel Media: Madeleine Norton

- BET: J. P. Lespinasse
- Bluefin Labs: Deb Roy, Anjali Midha, and Tom Thai
- Boxee: Andrew Kippen
- Bravo: Lisa Hsia and Maile Marshall
- Cablevision: Ben Tatta
- Canoe Ventures: Arthur Orduna and David Grabert
- Comcast: Mike Flanagan, Andrew Ward, and Thomas Straszewski
- DISH: Caroline Horner
- eMarketer: Lisa Phillips and Clark Fredricksen
- Facebook: Elisabeth Diana and Sarah Personette
- Fav.tv: Saverio Mondelli
- Forrester Research: James McQuivey
- GetGlue: Alex Iskold and Fraser Kelton
- GigaOM/NewTeeVee: Janko Roettgers
- Google: Rich Bertodatti and Kate Rose
- IntoNow: Adam Cahan
- INVIDI: Michael Kubin
- Knowledge Networks: Dave Tice
- *Lost Remote:* Cory Bergman and Natan Edelsburg
- Mashable: Christina Warren
- Microsoft Xbox: AnnMarie Thomas and Gaetano Bavaro
- Miso: Somrat Niyogi
- NBC: Julie DeTraglia
- NBC.com: Dana Robinson
- NBC News: Ryan Osborn and Ashley McCollum
- Nielsen: Jon Gibs and Radha Subramanyam
- PepsiCo: Shiv Singh
- PHILO: David Levy
- Roku: Chuck Seiber and Tricia Mifsud
- SecondScreen Networks: Seth Tapper and David Markowitz
- Snapstick: Rakesh Mathur and Lil Mohan
- Shazam: David Jones, Rica Squires, and Casey McDevitt
- SocialGuide: Sean Casey and Erika Faust
- Social TV Summit: Andy Batkin

- The CW: Allison Tarrant and Brian Doherty
- TiVo: Tara Maitra
- Trendrr: Mark Ghuneim and Alex Nagler
- TV Guide: Christy Tanner
- Twitter: Chloe Sladden, Robin Sloan, and Kristen Hawley
- YuMe: Frank Barbieri and George Sargent
- USA Network: Jesse Redniss and Suzanne McGee
- *Variety:* Andrew Wallenstein
- Viacom Media Networks: Jacob Shwirtz
- *VideoNuze:* Will Richmond
- Visible World: Claudio Marcus
- Yahoo!: Russ Schafer, Kryssa Guntrum, and Chuck DeSnyder
- The Weather Channel: Pete Chelala and Melissa Medori

We also featured seven end-user stories throughout the book and we want to thank Ilan Benatar, Chris Brum, Ezra Englebardt, Nina Perez, Chris Poulos, Brandon Stratton, and Olen Weaver for letting us capture a peek inside their colorful television lives.

Special Acknowledgments from Mike

If it were not for John Wall (@johnjwall), who connected me with Wiley, this book would not have happened as quickly as it did. John, along with C. C. Chapman (@cc_chapman), Steve Garfield (@stevegarfield), and Mitch Joel (@mitchjoel) each gave me helpful nuggets of advice at the onset of this project. There is a bit of fun irony in that I met all four of them through social media.

Two of my close friends, Michael James and Jamie Scheu, have been incredible sounding boards. Michael happened to pay me a visit the day I decided that I wanted to write a book about social TV. Jamie gave me invaluable feedback on the initial version of my proposal to Wiley and loaned me a book he bought on writing query letters. If I had any self-doubts about being the right person to author the first business book on social TV, they knew exactly what to say to keep my head fully in the game.

I owe a lot of gratitude to Adam Cutone, who sacrificed most of the 2011 sailing season with me so that I could focus on writing during any and all free time I had outside of work. I will not forget the many surprise home cooked meals and the altruistic understanding he showed along the way, often saying, "I know how important this book is to you."

To my family, especially my dad, the late Jerry Proulx, who taught me at a very young age why hard work and relentless discipline always lead to great outcomes. And to my mother, Anita Proulx, whose unwavering courage and childlike curiosity constantly remind me that life is a giant adventure filled with moments to be seized. In the parental "luck-of-the-draw," I feel like I won the grand prize.

Special Acknowledgments from Stacey

I want to thank my husband, Dimitry Herman, who played so many roles for me throughout this process, from legal advisor to editor and motivator. To my kids, for understanding why Mom always had her laptop out on the soccer field and had to do her homework while they were doing theirs.

I also want to thank my network and DRTV buying teams at Hill Holliday for their support and willingness to help with anything I needed. And to my family, friends, and colleagues, whose initial shock at me taking on this project turned to incredible support and encouragement.

About the Authors

Mike Proulx has spent the last 16 years working at various digital media and high-tech companies on the agency-side, client-side, and as an entrepreneur. His love of technology started when he was introduced to computers as a fourth grader in 1982 learning to program BASIC on a Radio Shack® TRS-80™.

Mike's career has constantly found him at the center of early and radical shifts in the media landscape. In 1996, Mike helped launch an online search engine at a company that had been focused on CD-ROMs. In 2000, he oversaw the development of then-nascent rich media websites for the entertainment industry. And in 2007, Mike was working in social media well before it became a part of our common lexicon.

At Hill Holliday, Mike oversees digital strategy and social media for the agency's roster of clients with an eye toward interconnecting media channels. Turning media on its side to create new experiences fascinates Mike. His passion for Web plus TV convergence led him to conceive, produce, direct, and cohost Hill Holliday's TV*next* summit in January of 2011. A frequent speaker, Mike has also contributed to a number of publications, including *BusinessWeek*.

Mike's client experience spans an extremely diverse set of vertical industries, including brands such as Warner Brothers, Columbia Tri-Star, AMC, IBM, Chili's, CVS/pharmacy, Novartis, Cigna, Dunkin' Donuts, Major League Baseball, TJ Maxx, Marshalls, and HomeGoods.

Mike earned his Bachelor of Science degree in Business Administration from the University of New Hampshire in 1995 and his Master of Science in Computer Information Systems from Bentley College in 2002.

You can follow Mike on Twitter at @McProulx or via his blog at www.mikeproulx.com.

Stacey Shepatin leads Hill Holliday's national broadcast buying practice, which involves directing the strategy, recommendation, and implementation for all national television buying and direct response advertising for Hill Holliday's portfolio of clients.

In 2010, Stacey led the formation of the Strategic Media Partnership Group, where she manages a multidisciplinary team and creates cross media programs for her clients.

Stacey is a lead negotiator on the Magna Global Advisory Council and is a member of the 4A's National Television Committee.

This past year, Stacey lead the agency's efforts for (RED) during their World AIDS Day Campaign, which won an Ad Club Media Maven award for best Media Plan with Spending under $1 million. In 2003, Stacey was named an Advertising Age Media Maven.

Stacey is a 1990 graduate of Colgate University, where she received a Bachelor of Arts in Economics and was the captain of the varsity softball team. She lives in Boston with her husband and three children, and enjoys playing tennis in her free time.

Introduction

The World of Tomorrow ▬▬▬▬▬▬▬▬▬▬▬▬

On Thursday, April 20, 1939, Radio Corporation of America President David Sarnoff announced the dawn of commercial television in the United States. Sarnoff's remarks described the medium as "a new art, so important in its implications, that it is bound to affect all society."[1]

His address strategically took place 10 days before the opening ceremony of the New York World's Fair. Themed as "The World of Tomorrow," the RCA-owned National Broadcasting Company fittingly transmitted US President Franklin D. Roosevelt's keynote address over the airwaves, marking the official birth of regularly scheduled television broadcasts in the United States.[2]

With much public allure surrounding this new medium, *Popular Mechanics* featured an article by Mr. Sarnoff in its September 1939 issue, simply titled, "The Future of Television." Underscoring the importance of content in the pioneering world of TV, Sarnoff wrote, "Let us consider next what sort of programming material television may present to its audience."[3] Throughout the many decades to come, writers and producers rose to the challenge to create programming that entertained and touched television audiences by providing them with a temporary escape from the often stark realities of the world outside of their living rooms.

Many remember watching Lucy and Ethel try to wrap chocolate candies off of a speedy conveyor belt on September 15, 1952 in what is today a classic *I Love Lucy* moment.[4] Forty-four percent of households tuned in to *The Beverly Hillbillies* on January 8, 1964 to see Granny chase a kangaroo around the Clampetts' home in "The Giant Jackrabbit" episode.[5]

Audiences were in tears by the dramatic story told in *Roots*, an eight-part miniseries that made its debut on January 23, 1977.[6] *The Cosby Show*'s young Rudy Huxtable endeared us when she lip-synched Margie Hendricks on October 10, 1984.[7] "Yadda Yadda Yadda" is forever ingrained in our common lexicon thanks to the hilarious April 24, 1997 episode of *Seinfeld*.[8] And millions of viewers watched a star be born on September 4, 2002, as Kelly Clarkson was named the very first *American Idol*.[9]

Television has produced countless resonant moments throughout its history. Even those who have not been moved or affected by a TV series have most certainly been impacted by watching events, news, or sports unfold across their screens. As Sarnoff wrote in 1939, "With the advent of television, the combined emotional results of both seeing and hearing an event or a performance at the instant of its occurrence become new forces to be reckoned with." But TV shows, events, news, and sports are not the only content on television.

TV Advertising Can Resonate Too

A television commercial is also content that has the potential to evoke resonance. The phrase, "I cry at Hallmark commercials" is a common and familiar one. It is hard to forget the 1979 Coca-Cola ad featuring a disgruntled Mean Joe Greene limping his way down a football stadium ramp. After being given a bottle of Coke from a young boy, the Pittsburgh Steelers defensive player gently tosses his football jersey to him saying, "Hey kid. Catch."[10]

We were similarly heartened in 2011 by a young "Darth Vader" trying to exert his telekinetic powers on a series of objects in and around his house: the exercise bike, the family dog, the washer and dryer, a baby doll, and even his sandwich. To his extreme disappointment, "the Force" did not seem to be strong within him. But then his dad, arriving home from work, pulls up his Volkswagen Passat into the driveway. A reinvigorated "Vader" seizes the opportunity to give his powers a go just one more time. As he channels all of his concentration and might while extending and pointing his arms toward the front of the car, the ignition suddenly fires (thanks to Dad using the remote starter). Our adorable Darth Vader is visibly shocked that, from his point of view, the Force came through for him after all.

The resonance of this particular Volkswagen TV commercial drove people online to experience it again and to share it with others. The official VW YouTube upload has generated over 45 million views[11] and is a great example of how the Web and television are complementing versus competing with one another.

The Internet Did Not Kill Television

While many people have proclaimed the death of television, the over-70-year-old medium is as healthy and alive as it has ever been. In fact, we are watching more television than ever before. According to research company Nielsen, the average American watches just over 35 hours of television per week,[12] in spite of the rise in online and mobile video viewing. The Internet has not killed TV; it has actually become its best friend. It is a companion for the growing masses of television viewers who are simultaneously going online while tuning in to their favorite shows.

The Web, social media, and mobile are rapidly converging with television and affecting the way in which we experience programming. David Sarnoff wrote a prophetic statement in 1939: "Television will finally bring to people in their homes, for the first time in history, a complete means of instantaneous participation in the sights and sounds of the entire outer world."

Over seven decades later, we are facing a period of déjà vu. Social media has created a new and powerful "backchannel" that is fueling the renaissance of live broadcasts. Mobile and tablet devices allow us to watch and experience both on-demand and live television whenever and wherever we want. And "connected TVs" blend Web and television content into a unified big screen experience—once again, at the center of our living rooms.

Although the television industry is undergoing a grandiose state of flux, it is also in the midst of one of its most exciting time periods; the outcome of which will only make TV more compelling, more interactive, and more accessible. And while the way in which we experience television continues to evolve, the medium is here to stay. The rise of a new medium does not always mean the end of another.

What Does This Mean for Television Advertising?

Just as television is changing, so is its advertising. The blending of media channels has created new opportunities for marketers to reach and engage with their target audiences. And this shifting television landscape is not just affecting advertising creative, but also how agencies plan and buy media.

Brands can no longer simply consider the program that is being broadcast on the television set; to do so is myopic and frankly, shortsighted. They must instead look at the larger cross-channel media experience that occurs nowadays with TV audiences in order to maximize their brand's impact within an ever-increasing distracted world.

The core of social TV starts with the backchannel, which is why we begin the book here. This is comprised of the millions of public conversations happening online while television programming airs. Brands who find ways to align themselves with or be a part of the backchannel unlock an entire audience with whom to engage.

Following Chapter 1, the next chapters are sequenced in the order in which audiences tend to experience television. Chapter 2 tackles the quickly evolving social TV guide landscape and examines how individuals discover what to watch in the modern era of television. Once one knows what he or she is going to watch, they may use any myriad of TV check-in apps that are growing in numbers and features, as illustrated in Chapter 3. Chapter 4 builds from our backchannel chapter and dives more deeply into the second screen experiences that television viewers have while watching TV. We discuss the concept of "synchronized applications" here, which provide opportunities for synched advertising.

Starting with Chapter 5, we examine what happens after a TV episode concludes to investigate the correlation between social media engagement and television ratings. We look not just at the TV shows themselves but also how to measure "social ratings" for TV commercials. Chapter 6 addresses the engagement with television shows that happens in between their episode airings—something we call "bridge content." When executed well, this can be a welcomed and ripe territory for branded entertainment.

Chapter 7 begins to take a turn in the television landscape with addressable advertising. The ability to target television commercials to eliminate any wasted impressions is the Holy Grail for brands. Chapter 8 gets us outside of the living room and illustrates the portability and accessibility of television that exists thanks in large part to mobile and tablet devices. Chapter 9 tackles the notion of Web plus television convergence head-on to bring to light the opportunities for brands within the connected TV world.

Our book concludes with a case study that ties all of the previous chapters together. We also illustrate how the blending of media is only going to continue making it that much more complex for brands to navigate. Given this, we highlight specific advice to advertisers from several of the industry leaders we interviewed to round out the chapter and the book.

Cutting to the Chase

The punch line of the book is a simple one—and it all points back to content. As it relates to television, people want to talk about and share the programming (including advertising) that resonates the most with them. Social media cannot and will not save a bad show or make poor products and services "look good." But social media absolutely has a powerful amplification effect in the presence of resonant content. And the evidence of this exists right before our very eyes in the millions of social impressions that comprise television's backchannel.

Scan for More

Scan this QR code using your mobile device for videos and visuals of the examples referenced throughout this section.

Don't have a smartphone with a QR reader app? No problem. You can access companion content directly by going to http://www .socialtvbook.net/tagged/introduction.

The Backchannel

*Bringing the Social
Conversation to the
Forefront*

On Sunday, February 9, 1964, The Beatles appeared for the first time on television sets across America.[1] Seventy-three million people tuned in to *The Ed Sullivan Show* at eight o'clock, Eastern Time, to experience the fresh sounds of the hugely anticipated British rock band broadcasting live from New York City on the CBS television network.

As the iconic curtain rose for the 779 time,[2] Ed Sullivan welcomed his viewers with news that The Beatles had just received a wire from Elvis Presley wishing them "tremendous success in our country."[3] The 728 audience members, watching the events unfold in person from CBS-TV Studio 50, erupted with loud applause and cheers.

Ed Sullivan took his spot on stage following a commercial break and exclaimed five simple words that would trigger a release of the pent-up excitement of over 23,000 US households: "Ladies and gentlemen, The Beatles!" Hysterical screams ensued and held for eight seconds before "All My Loving" (sung by Paul McCartney) kicked off the first of two sets.

It was during the second song, "Till There Was You," when each of the "Fab Four" was introduced via an onscreen lower third overlay of their first name displayed in bold white block letters. "PAUL" was the first to be introduced and was quickly followed by "RINGO" and then "GEORGE." As the camera panned over to John Lennon, his name came with a subtitle that read, *"SORRY GIRLS, HE'S MARRIED."*[4]

This episode, which aired during *The Ed Sullivan Show*'s seventeenth season, ranks among the most watched primetime broadcasts in US television history.[5] As Sullivan proclaimed, "Tonight the whole country is waiting to hear England's Beatles." While most of America indeed tuned in, the TV viewing experience was relegated to the living room in 1964. Coviewing was therefore defined in terms of whatever family members or friends happened to be watching and sitting right next to each other.

Hundreds of thousands of simultaneous discussions occurred during that infamous Sunday night. Viewers reacted to the events on their TV screens as they unfolded in real-time over the course of the 60-minute show. Yet those conversations were contained within the households in which they took place, and in the hallways and around many watercoolers at offices throughout the country on Monday morning. What were the raw, in-the-moment reactions to unexpected turns like the witty John Lennon lower third or message from Elvis? We will never really know for sure beyond viewers' firsthand accounts and reminisced anecdotes.

Television and Social Media Have Blended

Of course, 1964 was over four decades ago—four decades before TV viewing audiences started tweeting on Twitter and posting status updates to Facebook. Fast-forward 47 years to today's modern television experience, and you'll find that social media has given birth to a real-time "backchannel" made up of the millions of living, organic social expressions that act as a participatory companion to our favorite TV broadcasts. It exposes the conversations taking place in our once-isolated living rooms and connects households around the world into a single, opt-in, coviewing event.

Social media has become one of the highest cousage mediums with TV.[6] The portability of today's laptops, coupled with the steady rise in smartphone and tablet adoption, has made cozying up on the couch and being connected to the Internet in front of the television not only in vogue, but also a very natural and comfortable part of the TV experience.

Forrester Research reports that a survey of close to 3,000 US online adults revealed that 48 percent claim to use a personal computer while watching TV to chat, browse, or research what they are watching.[7] As the number of people engaging within social media continues to increase, the amount of online conversations about television *while* shows are airing within those platforms also increases.

Meet the Backchannel

The next time you tune in to television during its original airtime (versus watching something you have recorded on your DVR), type the name of whatever TV show you are watching into Twitter's search box at http://search.twitter.com. You will see staring right back at you the raw, real-time, and unfiltered stream of consciousness of the most basic version of television's backchannel. Twitter has become an integral outlet for TV viewers who are looking to express themselves while watching broadcasts of their favorite television programs.

Online conversation happens about a given TV show before, during, and after one of its episodes airs. Television's backchannel, however, is defined as the real-time chat that is happening within social media channels *during* the time that episode is broadcast. Consider it the additive subtext that connects you into a giant virtual coviewing party.

For example, when the Britney Spears episode of hit television program *Glee* aired on Fox in September of 2010, the backchannel produced over 285,000 tweets about the show.[8] That was back when Twitter averaged about 90 million tweets per day and was just shy of 5 percent of registered American users.

As of July 2011, the Twitter community is producing over 200 million tweets per day[9] and in September of 2011, Twitter announced it reached 100 million active users.[10] The 2011 Women's World Cup final broke a seven-month-old tweets per second record.[11] Seven thousand one hundred ninety-six tweets were created on the backchannel in just one second at the end of the soccer game, which was a live television broadcast.

This record was trumped 42 days later by Beyoncé's now-infamous baby bump reveal at the 2011 MTV Video Music Awards.[12] After her performance of "Love On Top," Beyoncé soaked in the audience's applause, tossed her microphone onto the stage, unbuttoned her purple sequined blazer, and showed the world she was pregnant. Eight thousand eight hundred sixty-eight tweets burst into the Twitter backchannel over the course of a single second and spread like wildfire as people across the globe shared the news. In effect, the Twitter backchannel is like an electrocardiogram (EKG) of television's heartbeat.

The Backchannel Is More Than Twitter

The average person has "liked" at least six television shows on Facebook. With over 800 million active monthly users worldwide—30 percent of whom are in the United States[13]—Facebook is as much a part of the real-time conversation around television as Twitter is. The big difference, however, is that the large majority of Facebook profiles are set as private and therefore bound by the interconnections of Facebook friends only. Yet there are a growing number of ways for communities of interest to publicly connect into the backchannel using this social network.

A defining moment for Facebook within the TV space happened when two engineers mashed up a newsfeed stream with a video viewer. This laid the groundwork for Facebook's live stream box application piloted during the 2009 presidential inauguration on CNN.com. The result was close to 27 million unique live streams served.[14] Those watching the video stream were able to post Facebook status updates directly from the streaming player and toggle between updates from everyone posting or those just from friends.

Among the Facebook and TV network partnerships that ensued includes a special edition of *Meet the Press*, which aired on January 8, 2012, just two days before the New Hampshire primary election. As host David Gregory moderated the debate amongst Republican presidential candidates, the show was simulcast on the

Meet the Press Facebook page. Viewers on Facebook were able to interact and share their questions while following the backchannel conversation as the debate was happening.

Twitter Gets More Attention

> *To do some of the most interesting, innovative stuff in television today, you actually don't need any new devices; you don't need any new apps or crazy fiber optic infrastructure. What you need is the will to produce TV in a new way.*
> —Robin Sloan, Content and Programming at Twitter, Inc.

Twitter's simplicity and easy access to its data tends to garner it more attention than any other platform within the social TV space. Its completely open and public nature makes any barriers to participation essentially nonexistent. One does not even need to have a Twitter account to view a given tweet stream. As (former) Twitter's Robin Sloan pointed out to us, "One of the things that's very important to any kind of interactive TV technology or platform is that people know the vocabulary and what they're supposed to do. If you have to give people the instruction manual before every experience, it's not going to work. With Twitter, you can put a hashtag on screen or an @ handle and people know what you're talking about. They know what that is. I think it's that simple recognition that makes it so incredible."

According to a *TV Guide* research study, 50 percent of Twitter users discuss the shows they are watching on television, versus 35 percent of Facebook users.[15] When doing the math, it should be noted that the active worldwide Facebook community outnumbers the equivalent Twitter user-base by about eight times. While the behavioral propensity to share TV experiences might be greater on Twitter, the sheer number of people who share ends up being larger on Facebook.

However, the study neither addressed the volume of television content shared comparatively between the two social networks nor weighed their relative amplification effect. Yet the point remains the same: The masses have taken to social networks to share their TV experiences as their favorite shows air ingraining a new and common behavior in TV viewers everywhere.

The Backchannel Is Reviving Live TV

The fact that you can interact on a different level with someone on Facebook or Twitter or get feedback from stars and experience information coming back to you on the second screen is driving a lot more people to return to watching television shows as they air.
        —Christina Warren, Entertainment Editor at Mashable

There is no doubt that social media amplifies the feeling of being connected and part of something bigger when watching television. In an interview with the *Wall Street Journal*'s Kara Swisher,[16] *Modern Family* creator Steve Levitan mentioned how he and his writers monitor the Twitter backchannel during new episode airings of his show. They are able to get a sense of which lines they wrote resonated the most by reading the real-time "Twitter laughter" that appears in 140-character tweets at a time.

While the experience of a highly engaged, lean-forward community is a compelling carrot to entice television viewers to return to the behavior of tuning in to television as it airs, the real motivating stick might be the fear of content spoilers. Twenty percent of TVGuide .com users reported that they are watching more live television broadcasts because they do not want the potential of people within their social networks to ruin the plots of their favorite shows.[17]

Viewers on the West Coast who fell victim to the time-zone tape delay of the 2011 *Grammy Awards* took to social media en masse to blame that same medium for spoiling the broadcast.[18] Winners, inevitably, ended up trending on Twitter as East Coast friends and followers posted updates three hours before a good portion of America was able to tune in.

This poses a dilemma for television networks in the age of social media and the real-time Web. Content can no longer be contained within time zones. The backchannel has shattered geographical boundaries in a very open, public, and mass reach way. A single tweet containing a spoiler could amplify and spread to hundreds of thousands, if not millions, of people in a matter of hours, if not minutes.

In April 2011, the BBC broke new ground when they decided to air the latest season of *Doctor Who* in the United States on the same day that it premiered in Great Britain.[19] In the past, the delay window between countries was a minimum of a couple of months, causing anxious Americans to seek out and watch copies of the show that were illegally uploaded online. So while social media was spoiling the content, the Web-at-large was actually distributing it.

Television Networks Have Embraced the Backchannel

It's so easy to forget that five years ago TV producers used to be scared about mentioning a URL on air that, somehow, it would be a distraction to the audience. Now there is a real feeling that social and digital is making what we're doing on television all the stronger.
—Ryan Osborn, Director of Social Media at NBC News

For the first time in 30 years, the 2010 *Emmy Awards* television broadcast had no West Coast time delay. Not only did host Jimmy Fallon integrate viewer tweets into the live broadcast; but NBC parallel broadcasted backstage video online using streaming service Ustream, which has a native Twitter and Facebook "social stream" backchannel integration. The embedded streaming player across various NBC online properties helped to amplify the backchannel conversation and increase their overall reach.

One of the first television networks to bring buzzworthy innovation to the backchannel was MTV, dating back to the 2009 Video Music Awards. In partnership with social media monitoring company, Radian6 and Stamen Design, MTV created a real-time Twitter tracker that visually depicted the volume of tweets about each celebrity by the size of their respective headshot. As the VMAs TV broadcast progressed, the array of celebrity headshots each separately expanded and contracted as the conversation about them increased and decreased.

The climax of the visualization experience was when country music star Taylor Swift was awarded Best Female Video, and Kanye West hijacked her acceptance speech. Back on the visual Twitter tracker, the headshots of both Taylor and Kanye dominated the second screen as the backchannel exploded with tweets about the incident. A visual Ping-Pong match ensued for a brief moment as their respective headshots took turns jockeying for screen real estate until Kanye's headshot practically enveloped the entire screen.

There was a staggering amount of Twitter activity about the incident taking place on the real-time backchannel. In fact, there were close to two million tweets over the course of the two coastal VMAs broadcasts—which, at the time, ended up tripling Twitter's average tweet volume.[20] The day after the broadcast, MTV.com had its second highest record number of visitors ever.[21]

The Backchannel Gets Armed with Filters and Visuals

The success of MTV's pilot backchannel visualization during the 2009 Video Music Awards led them to enhance and expand the concept for the 2010 Movie Awards broadcast—which produced even greater engagement results. The network has since brought the backchannel to life visually for all of its televised award shows.

Toward the end of 2010, Bravo launched its version of a Twitter tracker, aptly called the "@Bravotv Tweet Tracker." Users are able to easily segment the Twitter conversation by TV show and then drill down and engage with individual tweets about that show. The entire experience is embedded into Bravo's website and wrapped within a compelling—and even somewhat addicting—user experience. The elegance of Bravo's solution is that it is *always on*, which provides round the clock backchannel engagement for the network's diehard fans.

TV Shows Realize the Power of the Hashtag

It is becoming commonplace and best practice for TV shows to display onscreen Twitter hashtags. This serves as both an acknowledgment that there is already a backchannel conversation taking place on Twitter, as well as an instructional prompt for viewers to join in by tweeting their own thoughts. It creates a backchannel amplification effect with a very simple execution.

Comedy Central displayed a persistent #comedyawards hashtag in the lower left corner of the TV screen throughout the duration of its two-hour Comedy Awards show. Many of the Fox network shows are now sporting individual hashtags including #Glee. And viewers tuning in to the summer 2011 HBO season premieres were met with show name hashtags appearing on new episode previews that effectively prompted them to tweet about the given program on the backchannel.

Twitter has found through their own analysis—after having conducted numerous television integrations—that there is an immediate 2 to 10 times increase in the number of backchannel tweets created about a given TV show when an onscreen hashtag is included in the broadcast.[21]

Our Tweets Are Becoming Television Content

Two pioneering TV shows that integrated backchannel Twitter content directly into their actual television broadcasts are *Late Night with Jimmy Fallon* and *106 & Park*. One of the shows selects content in between episode airings, while the other does it live from the real-time backchannel. Both employ the use of various hashtags to elicit near instant responses from TV viewers and Twitter followers.

Late Night has found its groove with social media by reaching out to fans in a way that generates hilarious content for the show using actual tweet responses to fill-in-the-blank hashtags. Host Jimmy Fallon will introduce a hashtag topic on the previous night's broadcast and tweet it out—for example, #slapyourself. Show producers will then monitor the resulting tweet stream and pull a short list of their favorites. Jimmy will select 8 to 10 tweets to be read on his next show. The result is pure hilarity.

106 & Park, which airs weeknights live on BET, is reminiscent of a modern day version of MTV's *Total Request Live*—yet it is designed entirely around Twitter. As the network's most popular music series, various hip-hop and R&B music videos are requested via Twitter, and live artist interviews are featured. When on-air talent is introduced, their lower third onscreen display simply has their name and Twitter handle.

Everything about *106 & Park* epitomizes audience interactivity—not only with its live studio audience but also the show's virtual viewers via Twitter. Each day, the show introduces a new hashtag and features resulting tweets on a large interactive in-studio "Twitter board." For example, #NeverInAMillionYears produced thousands of tweets from loyal fans. *106 & Park*'s hashtags often end up trending worldwide on Twitter.

Television Talent Discovers Live Tweeting

The day Oprah Winfrey joined Twitter was the day the microblogging platform suddenly seemed mainstream. On April 17, 2009, Oprah tweeted for the first time—of course, she did it on her show. It was fitting that she had Twitter cofounder and then-CEO Ev Williams guiding her along the way: "HI TWITTERS. THANK YOU

FOR A WARM WELCOME. FEELING REALLY 21st CENTURY."
Despite the spelling error and all caps faux pas, this was yet another
milestone for Twitter—which was about to experience its share of
more celebrities joining.

During the broadcast of his premiere episode on CNN, host Piers
Morgan—who admitted to viewers that he had gone from hating
to absolutely loving and embracing Twitter—decided to live tweet
commentary while the taped show aired. "I'll be live tweeting during my 1st show tonight at 9pm ET in America, and then again at
8pm UK time tomorrow night." Watching the premiere while following Piers's Twitter stream gave viewers a bit of a peek behind the
curtain throughout his interview with—ironically—Oprah.

And a funny thing happened one Saturday afternoon in 2011
just two days before Valentine's Day. During an HBO rebroadcast
of the movie *Private Parts*, notorious radio personality (and star of
the movie) Howard Stern unexpectedly took to Twitter and began
tweeting from an insider's perspective: "the monologue on the
plane about carol alt was spontaneous. I just started talking into the
camera and there was only one take."

At first, a number of Howard Stern's Twitter followers were con-
fused as his tweets appeared almost rapid fire in their timelines
without any context. But once they caught on to the fact that Stern
was referencing his movie as a real-time commentary, they were
singing his praises and tuning in to watch HBO. Many tweeted back
saying they were glued to their seats as a result.

Apparently inspired by Howard Stern's Twitter stunt, *Survivor*
host Jeff Probst began live tweeting himself during airings of his
CBS reality show. "Don't forget—no DVRing Survivor tonight. Join
me LIVE as I tweet while we all watch the show together. It's a
global conversation."

Twitter analyzed the overall *Survivor* tweet volume from episode-
to-episode during the fall 2010 season of *Survivor* (when there
was no live-tweeting) and compared it with the spring 2011 season, when Probst became active on the Twitter backchannel. The
results were astounding. Most of the shows during the fall season

produced under 5,000 tweets per episode, whereas in the spring season the volume per episode was, in most cases, between 5 to 7 times higher.[22]

Social media creates the feeling of a more direct and intimate interaction between celebrities and their fans. This leads to a more engaged TV viewing audience who are increasingly abandoning their DVRs to tune in live. The lure of connecting within a community through a shared real-time experience is a compelling force.

But does the backchannel lead to ratings increases? In the case of *Survivor*, it did not. The show's spring 2011 season ratings were down across multiple demographic segments in comparison to the fall and the drop-off was most pronounced with younger viewers. Yet other shows—like MTV's VMAs and Movie Awards—continue to see ratings increases. (We take a much deeper dive on the correlation between social media and TV ratings in Chapter 5.)

Choosing Your Own Backchannel Adventure

The backchannel has evolved greatly from its fire hose roots. In June of 2011, Twitter rolled out a new version of its search feature—one that, by default, delivers the most algorithmically relevant information in the form of "top tweets." As Twitter's Director of Content and Programming Chloe Sladden points out:

> I am so excited that we're finally in a world where you can watch the Super Bowl and be on Twitter and have an algorithmically refined search without needing to do anything "extra." You just click on the hashtag #superbowl in a Tweet—which provides a far more compelling set of search results now. However, that is still only an algorithmic and universal experience; so the question becomes, what can a network do on top of that to shape it? Just because it's getting resonance doesn't mean it's the best complement to the TV broadcast. There's an

opportunity for producers to shape and mold the best Twitter-plus-TV experiences.

Networks have taken formal strides with television's backchannel that, while still open and public, offer viewers choices in making their backchannel experience a bit more personalized. After a successful trial-run in April of 2011, CBS hosted its second "Tweet Week" five months later—this time in promotion of its new fall television season. Each night during the weeks of September 12 and September 19, 2011, CBS featured one or two primetime series where fans could chat with talent from the given show who were live tweeting during the broadcast. The 11 selected series included *Hawaii Five-0*, *The Big Bang Theory*, and *The Good Wife*.[23]

The network upped the ante again during the week of November 6, 2011. Stars and talent from 23 various CBS television shows and events (including *How I Met Your Mother* and *Mike & Molly*) took over their respective show's Facebook page and Twitter accounts in what CBS called "Social Sweep Week."[24]

During the 2011 Primetime Emmy Awards on Fox, there was, of course, the official @PrimetimeEmmys Twitter account as the backchannel's emcee-of-sorts. But there was also *Glee*'s Lea Michele (@msleamichele) and *The Good Wife*'s Josh Charles (@MrJoshCharles), who live tweeted the event, sharing their bird's-eye view with everyone following them on Twitter. For those wanting a different backchannel experience, viewers could follow the likes of TV insiders James Poniewozik (@poniewozik), Jesse Fox (@JesseDavidFox), or number of others giving their flavor of #emmys commentary.

Putting All the Backchannel Components Together

NBC's *The Voice* premiered on April 26, 2011. The show's synopsis, at its ground level, was a reality-based singing competition. Following a series of on-air auditions, four celebrity musicians

(Adam Levine, Cee Lo Green, Christina Aguilera, and Blake Shelton) mentored contestants that performed live in front of a studio and TV viewing audience who cast votes for their favorite performances.

From a production perspective, *The Voice* was anything but ordinary; it broke new ground in the convergence of TV and social media. Show producers designed *The Voice*—adapted from a Dutch TV show—to have social media as its soul. On-air talent accessibility, openness, community, and connection were all tenets of the show's social media strategy. Their goal was to create a real-time coviewing experience that allowed spectators to become and feel as though they were part of the show. They succeeded by incorporating all of the best that the backchannel has to offer television.

#TheVoice hashtag was displayed on the broadcast screen—but unlike the Comedy Awards, it appeared only intermittently during strategic times when the Twitter backchannel conversation was most likely to amplify. Selectively displaying the hashtag made it behave in almost an alert-like fashion, which helped to mitigate the potential that viewers would tune out. As a result, 70 percent of the tweets about the show included its respective hashtag.[25]

The show's celebrity judges and host Carson Daly live tweeted consistently during episodes and commercial breaks. The program also established guidelines in advance that prohibited the on-air talent from tweeting any spoilers. Select backchannel tweets from both celebrities and the viewing audience appeared as lower thirds onscreen. Not only were people able to watch the show through the lens of the on-air talent; they were also able to experience the backchannel as integrated TV content.

The Voice producers instituted the concept of a backstage social media command center. When the show would cut away to the "V-Room," host Alison Haislip showcased trending topics and asked contestants questions selected from the backchannel on both Twitter and Facebook.

In addition to producing multiple worldwide Twitter trending topics as the show aired, the premiere episode of *The Voice* had eight times more conversation on the backchannel than the following night's *American Idol* broadcast and was the most discussed episodic TV show at the time—even beating out *Glee*.[26]

TV Shows Are Not the Only Backchannel Conversation Topic

During the Lost *series finale, a lot of the online chatter was about the Target ads and how they were so good because they were contextual back to* Lost.
—Geri Wang, President of Sales and Marketing at ABC

In June of 2006, Liberty Mutual launched a new marketing campaign to underscore the brand's core value of responsibility. The insurance company's TV commercials depicted a series of interconnected random acts of kindness set to the soundtrack of "Half Acre" by Hem. A toddler in a stroller drops her stuffed animal and a passerby stops to pick it up as the toddler's mother gives a glance of enormous, genuine gratitude. Later, as she buys something from the local bakery, she notices a patron's coffee mug is about to fall off the edge of the table at which he is seated—so she pushes it inward to avoid an accident. A man who happens to be standing at the coffee shop window notices the good deed and later helps a person up who has slipped and fallen on the wet sidewalk due to a downpour.

The pay-it-forward theme goes on for another six acts over the course of the 60-second TV spot. It resolves to a jogger who had earlier seen a man driving a pickup truck let a car pass through a gridlocked traffic jam. The jogger picks up a teddy bear that has fallen out of a baby carriage and places it back into the hands of the infant who dropped it. The camera pans up to the father pushing the carriage to reveal a familiar face. He is the person who performed the same good deed at the beginning of the commercial.

Thomas Okasinski, a retired engineer from Michigan, was so moved after seeing the Liberty Mutual commercial that he wrote and mailed the following letter, along with a modest check, directly to Liberty Mutual's Chief Executive Officer Ted Kelly:

Dear Mr. Kelly:
Kudos on your recent television advertisement, which depicts one act of kindness leading to another. I really love it.
In this age of TV comedy put downs, gratuitous sex and violence, negative political campaign advertising, it's refreshing to see something uplifting to the spirit. It makes your company stand above the rest.
While I cannot utilize any Liberty Mutual products at this time, please accept the enclosed check for use in your company's marketing budget or community service program as a sign of my gratitude.
Very truly yours,
T. Thomas Okasinski

At this point in 2006, there was no real-time television backchannel. Twitter was one month from its launch to the public and, similarly, Facebook was three months from opening itself up to noncollege students. However, a lack of social media did not change the fact that people wanted to share their feelings about the Liberty Mutual commercial. The underlying desire to connect and share has always existed within the human race. Social media simply enables our inherent behaviors and gives us an instant means to express ourselves to a world of other people.

So in 2009—when the now-vintage anthemic Liberty Mutual TV spot was dusted off and rerun during an episode of *Dancing with the Stars*—hundreds of tweets were instantaneously posted in reaction to the commercial. The backchannel had, for a moment, turned into a conversation about a TV advertisement from an insurance company, and not about the TV show that was aring.

"I am in love with the Liberty Mutual commercial that I just saw! Beautiful!"

"Anyone seen the new Liberty Mutual commercial? I'm not a fan of insurance companies but their commericial is fantastic!"

When content strikes a chord—even when that content is a television commercial—the backchannel harnesses and amplifies that resonance in the form of our real-time reactional tweets. Despite what some people have come to think, there is indeed still lots of life *during* the 30-second spot.

TV Spots Are Learning from TV Shows

Recognizing the opportunities within the real-time social Web, brands are now mimicking many of the emerging backchannel best practices pioneered by television shows into their TV commercials.

Audi was the first brand to display a hashtag within a television spot.[27] The luxury car manufacturer's 60-second ad aired during the 2011 Super Bowl sporting #ProgressIs toward the lower left corner of its ending art card. The on-air Twitter display, coupled with a paid 24-hour promoted Twitter trend using the same hashtag, significantly drove up the backchannel conversation about Audi and increased the brand's Twitter followers.

It just so happened that Audi saw record first quarter 2011 sales along with a rising demand within the United States.[28] Obviously, the backchannel cannot entirely take credit for this, but it played an important role in creating brand buzz and generating top-of-mind awareness in concert with a larger business and marketing strategy.

Brands are not only becoming enamored with Twitter hashtags displayed on their broadcast TV ads; they are also taking another cue from television programs by embedding tweets into TV commercial content. In fact, some advertisers are even creating TV spots *around* Twitter.

The Wheat Thins "Crunch Is Calling" campaign began airing during the summer of 2010. A large series of TV spots were produced based on a simple premise: Wheat Thins monitors Twitter and finds interesting tweets about the much-craved and beloved snack. Each TV spot features a single tweet where a camera crew and a spokesperson surprise the person who tweeted with some sort of stunt—in an almost *Candid Camera* style fashion.

In one of the Wheat Thins commercials from early 2011, the "Crunch is Calling" crew shows up to the house of Chris Macho—a man who had previously tweeted his excitement that Wheat Thins had begun to follow him on Twitter. They revealed to Chris a mobile billboard that would be driving around the rest of the day that read, "FOLLOW @CHRISMACHO. HE'S AWESOME!"

During the time period in which this version of the Crunch is Calling series aired, the Twitter backchannel conversation about Wheat Thins (and Chris Macho) more than tripled.[29] By using tweets as content within their TV spots, Wheat Thins was able to lift its brand conversation within Twitter itself.

The TV Spot Backchannel Conversation Gets Visual Too

It is no secret that for many people, the Super Bowl is as much—if not more—about the commercials as it is about football itself. This was precisely the impetus behind "Brand Bowl's" first appearance during the big game in 2010. A partnership between ad agency Mullen, social media monitoring company Radian6, and local news portal Boston.com, Brand Bowl measures and visualizes the Twitter backchannel about the Super Bowl ads as the game airs live.

The returning Brand Bowl backchannel conversation for the 2011 Super Bowl was visualized as a scoreboard. Each of the TV spots was stack-ranked in the order in which they were trending on the backchannel. As Twitter conversation amplified around a given commercial, its place on the scoreboard moved upwards.

The innovative part in how the rankings were done is that they were not just based on the amount of conversation; the scores also accounted for the given TV commercial's *sentiment*. The score was then calculated for each commercial by adding its number of positive plus neutral tweets, subtracting its negative tweets, and dividing by the total number of tweets for all of the commercials.

Chrysler's "Detroit" commercial was declared the overall 2011 Brand Bowl winner, although VW's "The Force" spot garnered the most positive sentiment. For that reason, some might argue that VW's ad *resonated* the most with audiences. All of this starts to get into the concept of social TV ratings and measuring TV spot engagement (which we address in great detail in Chapter 5).

Not All Marketing Impressions Are the Same

Social TV is a stunning phenomenon that marries relatively scarce (but high impact) social impressions to the massive scale of standard impressions that television has always been known for.
—Baba Shetty, Chief Strategy Officer at Hill Holliday

The familiar model of paid, owned, and earned media was designed from the marketer's point of view; it is certainly not how a consumer experiences media. As far as consumers are concerned, media impressions are either choice or nonchoice-based.

Nonchoice-based impressions result from a person's exposure to advertising that he or she did *not* actively seek out. A traditional TV or radio spot, print or online display ad, and an outdoor ad such as a billboard are all examples of nonchoice-based impressions. These impressions are highest in number and the ads that drive them tend to cast a wide net to the most mass—yet target-appropriate—audience possible. And while we are exposed to these impressions, we may or may not notice them. But when they do grab and hold our attention, the outcome can be quite powerful.

Choice-based impressions result from advertising which we *choose* to seek out and engage. Deciding to watch a video, clicking a search ad, typing a URL or hashtag shown in a TV spot, or selecting among a group of ads are each intended consumer actions. We are leaning forward when we engage with this kind of advertising and, therefore, our receptivity to a brand's message is at its peak. This makes the value of choice-based impressions worth a substantial amount to advertisers who can accomplish similar goals as using nonchoice-based impressions, but with a much lower volume and, arguably, higher impact.

A subset of choice-based impressions is *social impressions*. Every time we post, tweet, share, or "like," we generate impressions within our social networks. Social impressions are often received as an explicit endorsement from a friend, colleague, celebrity, or industry leader and are therefore the ones that influence us the most. Consider that the average account on Twitter has 349 followers, and the average number of Facebook friends is 130. Although not every one of your friends and followers will see every social impression you generate, many of them will. And then they may go on to multiply your social impression in turn by sharing it with others.

Now Is the Time for Marketers to Experiment with the Backchannel

Television's backchannel is filled with a constant stream of real-time social impressions. Some may live and die within the backchannel as quickly as they were created, while others will become amplified to reach more and more people. Many will be indexed by search engines and live forever to be discovered by hand-raisers' queries. Whichever the case, the backchannel is fertile ground for marketers. However, success only comes from having a posture of experimentation and integration.

For example, if your television commercial's content is one that has a naturally high propensity to generate positive conversation, showing a Twitter hashtag on-air will turbo-charge this conversation. Taking something that is a broad-reaching mass impression (the TV spot) and adding a simple, no cost prompt (the hashtag), will amplify your social impressions within the television backchannel. This increases both the reach and awareness of your brand message. Make the hashtag persistent for a good part of the duration of your TV spot. Audi's use of #ProgressIs within its Super Bowl commercial was pioneering; however, it flashed on the screen so quickly that it did not give TV viewers a chance to fully absorb it.

Consider as well running a promoted trend on Twitter using the same hashtag that is on your TV spot. A promoted trend appears at the top of the trending topics list on Twitter.com and is clickable to a promoted tweet from your brand's Twitter account. Brands do a media buy with Twitter to have their chosen hashtag displayed exclusively for 24 hours. This works particularly well when you have something newsworthy to share that will appeal to a broad audience.

Be mindful, however, if your brand has a disproportionate amount of negative sentiment or if your TV spot has little content that would prompt an inherently positive backchannel conversation. You do not want to inadvertently create a lightning rod that generates a rash of brand-bashing, spreadable, social impressions. Use social media monitoring tools, such as Radian6, to first gain perspective as to the existing social sentiment of your brand and the message you are looking to communicate in your TV spot.

Creating the 1 + 1 = 3 Cross-Media Effect

Look for ways to integrate your brand into the backchannel conversation during broadcast television tentpole events you sponsor. However, you must also be careful not to hijack the TV show's hashtag with advertising messages. Find ways for your brand's Twitter account to provide inherent value to the TV viewer by sharing content that relates to the show they chose to watch. Be part of the conversation on the backchannel—not an intruder who people might see as a spammer.

One brand that seamlessly integrated itself into television's backchannel is Verizon Wireless. During the opening of the 63rd Primetime Emmy Awards on September 18, 2011, host and *Glee* actress Jane Lynch sang a musical number as she paraded through a single building where all of television's fictitious characters supposedly lived. Going from room to room—or, rather, show to show—she eventually made her way into a high school gymnasium amidst a pep rally celebrating television.

As Jane navigated the crowd she ran into the infamous "Can you hear me now?" guy from the Verizon Wireless commercials, stopped to take a picture with him, and said, "Consider it tweeted!" Those who were also following the Twitter backchannel using the #emmys hashtag saw a promoted tweet and, by its nature, it was pinned as the first of the real-time search results. But the tweet was not from Verizon Wireless's Twitter account (although they paid for it). It was from Jane Lynch herself, and said, "Can you hear me now? We're on the #Emmys http://twitpic.com/6n32n7." The Twitpic was made to look like the picture that she took with the Verizon Wireless guy. What made the integration even more effective is that the official Verizon Wireless account retweeted Jane's tweet—thereby linking its own Twitter followers into a larger immersive cross-channel experience.

Television's Backchannel Is Fraught with Insights About Your Brand

Similar to the way in which *Modern Family* creator Steve Levitan and his writers learn about what lines resonate on the backchannel, so can you start to learn what people are saying about your TV commercials as they air. Social media is, after all, a giant unfiltered focus group—as a result, there are a lot of insights you can gain.

One way to start out is by setting up a Twitter search with your brand's name as the keyword on http://search.twitter.com while you are watching TV—especially if you have a prominent TV spot airing. Your brand's Twitter account could also engage in real-time with those who are tweeting about it. This is going to work best with highly resonant and high-impact television ad buys.

There is a goldmine of useful information that you can use to augment your traditional decision making inputs. Understanding what the lean-forward audience is saying about your content will only help as you fine tune your creative and messaging.

To help with this, there are a number of social media monitoring tools that can be used to conduct deeper insights and sentiment analysis on the backchannel conversation about your TV spots. This allows you to see results, after they air, in aggregate as well as drill down to individual TV spots for finer granularity. (Chapter 5 provides much more detail about this, using the concept of "social TV ratings.")

TAKE ACTION: THE BACKCHANNEL

Here are three key takeaways to consider when thinking about how your brand can get the most out of television's backchannel and increase your social impressions:

1. *Close the feedback loop.* Whether you are aware of them or not, TV viewers are having backchannel conversations about your commercials as they air. So at a minimum, actively monitor what people are saying about your brand; you will gain helpful insights as a result. When creatively appropriate, use your TV spot to direct people to the backchannel conversation as a means to amplify social impressions.

2. *Think* content—*not advertising.* The backchannel is no place for overt advertising messages. Rather, you want to build branded content experiences that naturally integrate with the backchannel's tone, tenor, and timing. Consider the backchannel as a source for content that can feed your creative and concept on a canvas that lies across channels and screens.

3. *Try, learn, and optimize.* The very nature of the backchannel is that it is *real-time.* So use its instant feedback mechanism to learn how your brand's unique qualities and social voice are best suited to participate. Maintain a "test and learn" attitude and collaborate with media partners to benefit from their lessons and emerging best practices.

It All Comes Back to Resonance

The backchannel responds the most to content that resonates—period. It is those moments of surprise and delight that we experience while watching TV that compel us to want to share our thoughts. As we end up generating lots of social impressions on the backchannel, it is possible that our engagement is helping marketers to produce better TV commercials. Just because a TV spot is an advertisement does not mean it cannot be great content.

Scan for More

Scan this QR code using your mobile device for videos and visuals of the examples and cases referenced throughout this chapter.

Don't have a smartphone with a QR reader app? No problem. You can access companion content directly by going to http://www .socialtvbook.net/tagged/chapter1.

2

Social TV Guides

Curating Social Media for Content Discovery

After graduating from Le Cordon Bleu College of Culinary Arts in Las Vegas, world wrestling fanatic Brandon Stratton moved to Austin, Texas, to begin his new career as a professional chef. Brandon first got into Twitter while promoting his fine dining restaurant. The 36-year-old long-haired, tattoo-sporting husband and father recently opened Sputnik, a traditional burger and hot dog joint in the hipster East 6th Street area of the city.

In lieu of a chef's coat, Brandon cooks his culinary masterpieces wearing death metal t-shirts and jeans. While his passion for sharing good food and love of the extreme side of music may seem like an unusual combination, Brandon built up a community on Twitter (despite his early doubts about the usefulness of the platform) of like-minded chefs who use the hashtag #foodporndeathsquad that Brandon created. Although he is (figuratively) strapped to his restaurant's kitchen for 12 hours at a time, when he does go home, Brandon is a TV junkie—one who is now addicted to engaging on the Twitter backchannel while watching his favorite shows, which include *The First 48*, *True Blood*, *Dexter*, and *The Walking Dead*.

One night in 2011, while Brandon was catching the latest broadcast of *WWE Monday Night Raw*, he noticed a tweet on the backchannel from former WWE writer and producer David Lagana (@Lagana). David's tweet contained a link to SocialGuide, an online television guide powered by the social media backchannel. Since Brandon values David's opinions about wrestling as both a thought leader and influencer (the best kind of "social impression"), he was curious to find out what SocialGuide was all about.

His first reaction, after clicking the Twitter link and visiting the SocialGuide website, was that it seemed "Kind of like a TV guide, but with people talking about stuff." And because of his existing fondness for the backchannel as a means to get into playful taunts with other TV wrestling fans, Brandon immediately downloaded the SocialGuide mobile app to his HTC EVO 4G smartphone.

Brandon recognizes that it is human nature to want to socialize with people having similar interests. Since his wife, a grocery store bakery manager, does not share his work hours, Brandon's social outlet has become his virtual coviewing television experience. It allows him to express his opinions about TV shows as a real-time conversation with a broad spectrum of people.

Brandon welcomes SocialGuide as an alternative to his Time Warner onscreen channel guide, because he finds it to be "10 times faster" when looking for TV shows. He likes how SocialGuide automatically presents the most social shows that are currently airing, versus having to scroll through hundreds of channels that he never watches just to try and find out when *Iron Chef America* is on, tune in, and let people know he is watching it. And because SocialGuide aggregates the Twitter backchannel through the app itself, Brandon often launches it on his smartphone while he's at work—just to check which shows people are discussing the most and browsing the conversation vibe to ensure he is not missing out on something good.

Brandon explains that he uses SocialGuide up to 30 times daily while watching television on his days off. The music industry-exec-turned-chef now prefers to tweet into the backchannel through SocialGuide since the application makes it easy to share. He likes having the "(via @Social_Guide)" stamp appended to his backchannel Twitter posts, since he feels that it provides something different than "just shooting out random tweets." He admits that since Twitter is embedded into the app, pure laziness is part of his motivation to also tweet from SocialGuide; he doesn't want to take the trouble of switching back and forth between the Twitter and SocialGuide smartphone apps.

Since Brandon does not have a DVR—and because of the nature of his job—his television time is normally relegated to windows that span from midnight to three o'clock in the morning, and 10 in the morning until noon. Because of his somewhat odd schedule, Brandon relies on SocialGuide as a way to help him easily find shows to watch. He enjoys the serendipitous nature of seeing shows bubble to the top of the app that he would never have remembered to even consider watching on his own accord.

A significant reason that Brandon engages on the backchannel through SocialGuide is that he finds it fun to have instant access to a massive group of strangers who are watching television at the same time. He hopes that by sharing what he is watching on Twitter using SocialGuide, someone following him might discover the show and start watching it too. After all, the backchannel was the way in which Brandon discovered SocialGuide, and now he cannot imagine watching television without it. As far as Brandon's concerned, the days of using the default cable system's onscreen channel guide are over.

A Channel Guide Is More Than Just a Program Listings Grid

TV Guide cemented its place in television history making the notion of a television broadcast schedule human. The weekly digest featured editorial, photos, and cover art that triggered powerful and directionally opposite emotions of anticipation and nostalgia. After buying up a number of regional television listings publications (the likes of which included *TV Forecast*, *TV Digest*, and *Television Guide*), Walter Annenberg created the first publication of national scale to provide television viewers with both broadcast and local TV listings.[1]

The first issue of *TV Guide* launched on April 3, 1953, and featured newborn Desi Arnaz Jr. front-and-center on the magazine's cover. A small headshot of Lucille Ball appeared on the cover's upper right-hand corner just below the headline "LUCY'S $50,000,000 BABY" in a red block typeface.

At a price of just 15 cents, *TV Guide*'s initial distribution encompassed 10 cities and sold 1.5 million copies in its first year. Growing to a circulation of 20 million by 1970 made *TV Guide* the largest weekly magazine in the world.

From its beginning, *TV Guide* established itself as the authority on television programming. The magazine's ever-popular fall preview issues were always an anticipated delight in subscribers' mailboxes. It was not uncommon for television viewers to scour each issue of *TV Guide* using a pen or highlighter (sometimes two different colors) to plan their personalized television schedule for the upcoming week.[2]

In its early days, *TV Guide*'s program listings were comparatively basic, as there were only three television networks in 1953: National Broadcasting Company, Columbia Broadcasting System, and the DuMont Television Network. In order to account for the differences in localized programming within various geographic regions, *TV Guide* published 180 local editions at its peak. While the articles and covers remained the same, it was, of course, the actual TV listings that differed across various editions.

The popularity of *TV Guide* issues as collectors' items due to the magazine's covers led the publication to begin experimenting with "split covers" in the early 1990s, following Rupert Murdoch's purchase of the company. For example, the January 26, 1991 issue of *TV Guide* had two different covers: one of them featured a photo of Cybill Shepherd to promote her upcoming TV movie, *Which Way Home*, while the other showcased the 25 most memorable Super Bowl moments in history.[3] Although the covers were different, the content inside was the same and included both feature stories.

However, two covers were not enough on August 24, 1996 when *TV Guide* celebrated *Star Trek*'s thirtieth birthday. The magazine created four different covers this time, each of which featured the "captain" of a different *Star Trek* TV series, including *The Next Generation*, *Voyager*, and *Deep Space Nine* in addition to the original *Star Trek* series.

While the magazine's debut issue is the most sought-after (and hence most expensive), several *TV Guide* back issues that sport vintage superheroes are at the top of collectors' lists. For example, the September 25, 1953 *TV Guide* features George Reeves as both Clark Kent and Superman. On the cover of the March 26, 1966 issue,

Batman (played by Adam West) makes a fighting pose, complete with the show's iconic "POW" exclamation. On April 26, 1958 *Zorro* fans saw their masked hero making his signature "Z" with his sword.[4]

As the number of television networks and cable channels continued to grow, it became much more logistically complex for *TV Guide* to print and distribute all possible permutations of program listings. It also became increasingly more navigationally cumbersome for readers trying to discover new shows. While advances in technology that gave way to the emergence of electronic programming guides (EPGs) solved both issues, it led to the demise of *TV Guide* itself.

By 2005, the magazine's circulation had dropped more than fourfold. After 52 years, *TV Guide* printed the last of its original digest-sized format on October 9, 2005. The final issue was published with one of nine different possible covers, each a modern day re-creation of classic *TV Guides*. For instance, Regis Philbin and Kelly Ripa replicated the 1966 *I Dream of Jeannie* cover; the cast of *Scrubs* appeared as the 1976 cast of *M*A*S*H*; and even Homer Simpson dressed up as *The Flintstones'* leading man Fred Flintstone, who had originally appeared on the popular June 13, 1964 *TV Guide* cover.[5]

TV Guide Magazine, as it is now called, is still in publication today. At a larger dimensional size and printing only two editions (instead of 140), the new *TV Guide* is very different from its digest-sized predecessor. Program listings have become relegated to a simple grid, and the magazine focuses predominately on editorial and commentary.

The Origin of the Electronic Programming Guide

Almost three decades after *TV Guide* was originally published, the first electronic program guide (EPG) became available in North America. Simply called "The Electronic Program Guide" in 1981, the service—developed by United Video Satellite Group[6]—provided its software to cable TV head-end master facilities, which in turn broadcasted the EPG as a dedicated cable channel.

Back then, the program guide rendered TV listings that automatically scrolled over the full television screen. A broadcast window of four hours displayed as 30-minute increments were available to view at any point in time during its continuous loop. A mainframe computer in Oklahoma transmitted program updates using a 2,400 baud modem as a communications link to each of the computers running the Electronic Program Guide.

The second half of the decade saw a number of improvements to the EPG. A 1985 software upgrade enabled cable companies to lightly customize how the guide was broadcast. In addition to setting the scroll speed, text-based ads could be inserted either as a banner along the bottom of the EPG or amidst its scrolling TV listings. In 1988, the EPG service was rebranded as "Prevue Guide"[7] and another software upgrade introduced the notion of a split screen. The channel grid became 50 percent its size and appeared on the bottom half of the split, while the top half of the screen supported video. This allowed viewers access to more dynamic content while they waited for the guide to cycle through all of the TV listings.

Come March of 1993, a major redesign of Prevue Guide updated the EPG's look, layout, and added closed captioning as well as VCR Plus+ logos (remember those?). Later that same year, Prevue Guide became known as "Prevue Channel"; it updated its hardware and—perhaps most notably—introduced short original content features as a means to draw an audience.

Toward the end of the nineties, United Video Satellite Group (who created and owned the EPG software) purchased *TV Guide*. Within a year, they were acquired themselves by Gemstar International Group. The "TV Guide Channel" was introduced in the midst of the acquisitions as Prevue Guide's new brand.

By the time the new millennium rolled around, the TV Guide Channel was offering full-length original programming, leading to its new name—"TV Guide Network," which made its debut on June 4, 2007. By 2010, the once full-screen channel guide that became half its size in the late eighties was now a simple one-line grid that occupied the bottom quarter of the TV screen. By this time, most television viewers had already made the shift to much more usable interactive programming guides (IPGs) on their set-top cable or satellite boxes.

Interactive Programming Guides Gave TV Viewers Control

There were obvious limitations to the original electronic programming guide—the most glaring of which was the amount of time that viewers were forced to wait until a block of channels one cared about scrolled into view. If an unexpected event like the phone ringing or the oven timer buzzing took a viewer's attention away from the screen, they would have to wait for the entire channel lineup to once again cycle through.

Along with the advent of digital set-top boxes came a new way for TV viewers to discover what was on television by actually interacting with the onscreen guide. What has become a very familiar user experience by today's standards, IPGs introduced the ability for television audiences to self-scroll, select, and click into deeper levels of information about a given show's episode, set program reminders, personalize TV listings, and change the channel from within the guide.

Of course, all of this constantly changing program data needs to come from somewhere. So in lieu of managing and maintaining it themselves, cable and satellite companies rely on third-party aggregators who handle all of the meta-data from updates to distribution. While there are a number of players in the IPG data space, Tribune Media Services is the nation's leading provider.[8] The company has a dedicated team of people whose sole job is to gather and organize the most recent TV meta-data from television programs airing on every network and local station.

Tribune Media's channel lineup database contains over 22,000 different channel maps for use by various cable, satellite, and phone companies—accounting for 2,700,000 television episodes. In addition to listings, schedule information, and channel lineups, Tribune's data feed also includes TV network logos and other photos. Microsoft, TiVo, Comcast, and Yahoo! are some of the companies that use Tribune as the source of their respective interactive program guides; not just for their set-top boxes, but also for their websites and mobile solutions.

The Internet poses a growing alternative for source data given the accessibility of and ease at which data can be integrated as an interoperable set of Web services.[9] Coined "electronic service guides" (ESGs), these feeds are comprised of a vast array of multimedia content and advertising[10] that can feed any number of devices including connected TVs, which we address in Chapter 9.

Increased TV Content Has Led to Decreased Programming Guide Usefulness

Because of the way people consume content these days, you have to be able to tell them what's on now, what's on their DVR, and what's available online via Netflix, Hulu, and other services—and bring that together in one, integrated place.
                    —Cory Bergman, Founder of *Lost Remote*

Back in 1953, when there were only three television networks, it was a pretty straightforward endeavor to find something to watch at any given point. Today, however, there are over 500 channels for TV viewers to attempt to navigate. Add to the mix TV shows from video on demand, DVR, Netflix, Hulu Plus, iTunes, and full episode players, and we end up with more television programming from which to choose than ever before. Yet in spite of so much choice, masses of people continue to complain, "There is nothing to watch."

The root cause of the issue is not a lack of good programming; instead, it is the need for a single source that viewers can use to simply discover and plan television content. The onscreen interactive program guide is reaching its usable limits. Despite its "interactivity," the IPGs linear features are becoming progressively less helpful in trying to find something to watch.

Additionally, an increasing accessibility of data has created opportunities for developers to invent the "next generation" television programming guide. Cory Bergman of popular social TV blog *Lost Remote* sees recommendations as the center point of the television screen:

> We're starting to get to the point where we have enough data so that someone who puts together a good algorithm could start suggesting really impactful stuff that people want to watch. When that happens, we'll get to a point where you won't just see the last channel you watched when you turn on your television set; instead, there will be a recommendations screen. And all of a sudden, that screen will become the most important and valuable and expensive real-estate in television.

Therefore, in the wake of an increasingly complex television landscape, the key to future programming guides' success is to be incredibly simple to use.

Is There Anything Simpler Than Word-of-Mouth?

If a person you completely trust tells you that you must watch a particular TV show, your propensity to tune in is likely to be extremely high. Similarly, if thousands of people on the backchannel are causing a television broadcast to trend, chances are that you are going to take notice.

Social media is fueling an alternative to the "traditional" programming guide to which eager TV viewers—as well as television networks—are turning. Twitter's promoted trends (in which an advertiser can purchase a hashtag that appears at the top of Twitter's trend list for 24 hours) was fraught with television show names during the 2011 fall season premiere. For instance, on September 22, 2011 the promoted trend for the day was #CharliesAngels, which linked to a promoted tweet from an ABC Twitter account for the series that read, "Go behind the scenes of ABC's new #CharliesAngels, premiering tonight at 8|7c on ABC! youtu.be/RZ91zEMTVFA." The idea behind using promoted trends is, of course, to spark the conversation about the show on Twitter before it airs—something that would hopefully lead to heightened awareness and ultimately, greater tune in.

All of these conversations—which take place within the real-time social web about television—deliver results in the form of massive amounts of data. The serendipitous nature of a one-off can certainly affect content discovery as individual tweets or Facebook posts. But what is even better is when the collective public social stream about TV creates a new way to look at what is on television.

Because of this, the market has become filled with a number of online guides looking to take advantage of the power of social media. It seems as though there is a new social programming guide (SPG, also referred to as a social TV guide) popping up once a month—each of which put their own spin and flair on matching TV shows to their respective audiences. The one common thread that runs throughout SPGs is that they all—in some way—leverage the power of community to cut through the content noise to surface relevant programming.

We do not attempt to identify every player within the entire social TV guide landscape within this chapter; such an undertaking would need much more time and space. Instead, we highlight a few key apps by way of showcasing the broad range of utility within this category.

SocialGuide Is Powered by the Backchannel

You turn on your TV and you go to the on-screen guide. That guide actually worked for consumers 30 years ago, when there were only 50 or a 100 channels, because you could actually scroll within four or five clicks to see what was on TV. Now there are 1,000 channels, and statistics show that half the people who have HD TVs don't even know what their HD channels are. We thought that adding social intelligence into an SPG format would be a good way for consumers to find out what's on television.

—Sean Casey, Founder and CEO at SocialGuide

SocialGuide launched in February 2011 after entering an R&D deal with none other than Tribune Media Services. Billed as the first real-time social guide for television, SocialGuide's ability to marry the backchannel to US television listings (thanks to Tribune's data) provides a compelling, new TV discovery tool and filter by which to surface the most social TV shows.

After downloading the SocialGuide app, first-time users are asked to enter their zip code and specify their cable provider. Based on this information, SocialGuide's intelligence engine creates a localized SPG that ranks shows in the order of their real-time popularity as measured by social impressions. For example, on a random Thursday night in the fall of 2011 (as this was being written), the top six most social shows according to SocialGuide were *The Big Bang Theory*, *The X Factor*, *The Vampire Diaries*, *Jersey Shore*, *Community*, and *Charlie's Angels*.

SocialGuide ingests information for 177 channels, accounting for all major broadcast networks plus the most popular cable channels. Since the application knows whether or not a given user is a digital television subscriber, it will display only high-definition channel rankings where applicable. This makes it incredibly easy to scan the rankings, discover a show, and know exactly what channel it is on.

The app enables users to filter program listings by genre and includes "reality" as one of the options. This is particularly helpful given that reality competitions tend to naturally produce a good share of backchannel conversation and SocialGuide creates a simple path by which to find them. Other genre filters include Series, Movies, Sports, and News.

A toggle "talk bubble" toward the top right turns on, displaying the most recent tweet about each show in the SocialGuide listings. This gives users a rough sense as to the type of backchannel conversation that is taking place for each of the shows without having to drill down into the app.

Clicking any show listing pulls up the full Twitter backchannel conversation for the selected TV program. Though the tweet stream displays tweets from everyone by default, users can easily filter it to only display friends who are tweeting about the show or those just from the cast members of the given TV series. Since SocialGuide has preconfigured and mapped all of the Twitter accounts for television celebrities and athletes, using this feature is a fun way to follow an ever-increasing amount of celebrity live tweeting, as we illustrated in the previous chapter.

SocialGuide makes it very easy for its users to post into the backchannel by auto-filling the status update field with a TV series' official Twitter hashtag. The app's design embraces the ability to switch back and forth from one TV show's backchannel conversation to another. Not only is this helpful for those users who like to channel surf; having the backchannel as such an integral part of the app also gives SocialGuide users instant access to a real-time data source that can help them decide whether or not to tune in to a specific program.

Yap.TV Brings the Notion of a Social TV Guide to the iPad

In August of 2011, Yap.TV launched the third version of its social TV guide available for the iPhone, iPod Touch, and iPad.[11] Touted as a "completely personalized TV show guide," the app also acts as a second screen experience that allows users to engage with content (such as polls) during a given show.

Yap.TV's iPad app has a stunning graphical user interface[12] that celebrates television through its simple and clean design. Its default display exhibits 20 shows in "guide view" that are rendered as large TV show art thumbnails, laid out five across and four down. Links for filtering toward the upper right corner of the screen allow users to narrow the number of shows displayed by a particular genre. An elegant slider-based navigational system at the bottom of the display shuffles TV program titles by specified day of the week as well as time of day.

More filters in the upper left-hand corner include the ability to display the top 20 TV shows based on an algorithm that accounts for social impressions. In addition, users can navigate to their list of favorite shows, as well as their Yap.TV friends' favorite shows. For less visual users, a "lineup" button displays the program guide as a more traditional channel grid while still employing all of the same time-based filtering features and functions.

Clicking into any show at any point reveals a quadrant-like preview display of available content about the given show including related tweets, a "Live Chat" option, polls, and photos. The Twitter integration on the iPad version of Yap.TV is particularly interesting. When selected, a side-by-side split screen shows two different tweet streams, and all "Fan Tweets" appear on the active left-side window by default. Tweets from the show's actors and/or official show Twitter account are segregated into their own stream on the right side. When users click, this window is activated and flip-flops with the Fan Tweets windowpane.

Similar to other social TV guides, Yap.TV also personalizes its channel lineup based on each user's specified pay TV provider. The app also supports the ability to follow other Yap.TV users who can enter into live chats about a given TV show.[13] In addition, the option to choose favorite television shows acts as a bookmark-of-sorts that gives Yap.TV users quick access to the pages for their

most beloved programs. Favorites also become a part of each Yap.
TV user's profile, which helps to tell the rest of the Yap.TV community who they are and what they like.

BuddyTV Combines Recommendations with the Power of the Remote

In July of 2011, the BuddyTV Guide app launched as a "universal guide"[14] whose goal is to have people watching what they want
in less than 20 seconds. In addition to serving as a television recommendations engine, the smartphone app also has remote control capabilities if paired with Google TV (a connected TV that we
describe in Chapter 9), the TiVo Series 3 set-top box,[15] or the AT&T
U-verse receiver.

BuddyTV's power lies primarily in its ability to constantly tune
its recommendations over time based on the actions a given user
takes within the app. These include tagging favorite shows by clicking a heart icon, rating shows on a one to five scale, and alerting
BuddyTV to the fact that you have tuned in to a particular show.
The more actions that one takes within the app, the better its recommendations become.

Users also have the option of connecting their existing Facebook
account into the app. This allows BuddyTV to ingest existing TV
show "likes" as yet another input to its personalized suggestions,
and lets users recommend TV shows to their Facebook friends.
Additionally, BuddyTV users can easily post Facebook status
updates about what they are watching, which further prompts
social content discovery.

Because users specify their cable or satellite provider upon initial setup, BuddyTV's suggestions include US television listings,
video on demand titles, and Netflix content when applicable.
Recommendations are displayed using TV show art thumbnails
and appear on the BuddyTV Guide's home screen under an "Airing
Now" label. Users can easily swipe through the artwork to browse

all of the suggestions that are currently airing on TV at the time they are using the app.

Appearing just below the Airing Now section are tabs that let BuddyTV users toggle between upcoming show recommendations as well as their favorites, most popular shows, and their personalized Watch List. Selecting a show from any of these groups provides details about the TV show's current or next episode airing. A user can also use this space to make the show a favorite and rate it, as well as post comments about the specific episode to their Twitter and/or Facebook profiles.

Additionally, an on/off switch button embedded within each show's profile page lets users add the given show to their BuddyTV Guide Watch List. Doing so sends push notifications prior to airings of the specified show, and increases its recommendations weighting. As a further means to ensure that users do not miss Watch List TV broadcasts, there is also an option that adds the show's airing day and time as an event within the user's default calendar on their smartphone or tablet device.

Fav.tv Focuses on the Before and After Part of the Television Experience

If you pick up a TV Guide *today, you'll probably struggle to find the pages where they have an actual guide of what's on television. Fav.tv is what* TV Guide *could have been had they just stayed true to their original solution of helping users find out what's on TV. As soon as you follow a show, fav.tv presents a customized guide that keeps viewers from having to flip through a bunch of* TV Guide *pages or go through a grid of 200 channels to figure out what's on tonight.*

— Saverio Mondelli, Cofounder and CEO at fav.tv

A relative newcomer to the social TV guide space, fav.tv launched on September 13, 2011 with an extremely simple user interface packaged around five buttons. "Activity" is, essentially, the fav.tv newsfeed that shows the actions that a user and their fav.tv community have taken within the app.

The "Queue" is akin to a "to-do" list for TV episodes. It displays shows that the user has opted to watch that they can check off as complete while answering a simple yes/no question as to whether or not they enjoyed the episode. "What's On" is the actual program guide itself, which can filter shows by all, preferred, or featured. The fourth button, "Shows," lists users' favorite TV programs. Finally, "Messages" are communications sent to and received from other fav.tv users.

The basic building block of fav.tv is the act of following a TV show, which places that show into the user's favorites with an option to "pin" it onto the home screen for one-click access. Any given show page lists upcoming episodes and other helpful curated information—including a link to its profile on imdb.com. There is also a tab that lists all episodes (including past seasons) for that particular show.

According to CEO Saverio Mondelli, fav.tv was designed to address TV viewers' needs before and after watching a television show:

> We have this philosophy that there are three important parts of TV. There's *the before,* during which you gather information to determine when a show is on and when and how you're going to watch it. Then there's *the during,* when you're actually watching the show. And then there's *the after,* where you have these random sporadic conversations—whether they be on Twitter or on Facebook or around the watercooler at work. Fav.tv focuses on the before and after.

An "Activity" tab on each TV program's show page toggles the user to all related comments from other fav.tv users. This acts as the hub of the social conversation from fav.tv community members around a given program. Mondelli feels this is a particularly compelling feature to use after an episode airs:

The after is the "social" part of social TV. It's the part that our competitors are encouraging you to do during the show. We find that when you're watching TV, you don't want to be talking; you want to focus. A perfect example of this is a show like *Lost*. Everybody had theories about the show and every episode opened new mind-sets and new ideas about what could be going on. People want a forum to put those ideas out there, get validation from other users, and hear what everybody else thinks. That's what *the after* is: going back to the community that you've established for yourself. We've built fav.tv so that you can establish a main network of your friends, family and people whose opinions you actually care about.

Fav.tv looks to differentiate itself from other social TV guides based on its simplicity and ease of use. A mere click of the "follow" button for a particular TV show is all of the user effort that it takes to engage in this platform. Fav.tv says that it handles the rest to ensure that its users will never miss out on another TV show again.

And the Story Comes Full-Circle to TV Guide

A challenge for consumers right now is that there are so many options and so many ways to watch . . . in some ways, it's overwhelming and difficult to manage. That is why TVGuide.com created our Watchlist product; we think there's an opportunity for us to help people manage what is a proliferation of content options, distribution methods, and delivery options for consumers.

—Christy Tanner, Executive Vice President and
General Manager at TVGuide.com

TVGuide.com has managed to grow its visitor traffic close to eight times what it had back in 2006 through constant innovation and online product development. With over 23 million unique monthly users to its website, the TV Guide brand remains trusted and strong.

During the summer of 2011, the site launched two products that upped the ante in the social TV guide space. TV Guide's Watchlist officially emerged in August of 2011 as a highly personalized, relevant, and social way to discover, plan, and track television shows. One month later, in September of 2011, TVGuide.com launched its Social Power Rankings product, which lists the most popular television shows based on activity that happens directly on TVGuide.com.

Within a month of its unveiling, TVGuide.com users had created over 375,000 Watchlists. Users can add shows, celebrities, and even sports teams to create their custom Watchlist, which allows them to see upcoming broadcast airings and watch the latest episode online (where applicable). With television consumption on the rise, the Watchlist is a helpful planning tool—as TVGuide.com EVP and General Manager Christy Tanner states:

> Every year, we ask people how many hours of TV are they going to watch. The percentage of people in our survey who said they are going to watch more than 30 hours of television a week went up this year to 32 percent from 28 percent last year. So more people are watching more hours of TV than ever before . . . because there are more and better options and so many ways to watch. If your goal is to just keep on watching more TV, the Watchlist can help you manage, with precision, the number of shows you can jam into a single day.

TVGuide.com includes an option to view Watchlists created by celebrities, which is yet another compelling and intriguing way to discover new content. The top 10 Social Power Rankings are tabulated from TVGuide.com's usage data that includes check-ins, user comments, episode discussions, and Facebook and Twitter posts initiated from the site. The rankings are not updated in real-time;

instead, TVGuide.com's editorial staff calculates and curates them. On this particular day, the top three shows within the Social Power Rankings are *All My Children* (due to the series finale), *Pan Am*, and *The X Factor*. An "add to watchlist" button appears next to each of the rankings, thus closing the content discovery loop from intrigue to action.

The Quest to Drive Tune-in

When the DVR came along, people said that it was basically going to kill television. It actually made people watch more because it made them watch smarter. Just wait until social TV guides can accurately recommend what people will want to watch. You'll see people consuming more content in a smarter way and they'll be more likely to share that content—which then feeds the whole system.

—Cory Bergman, *Lost Remote* Founder

All of the players in the social TV guide space have potential access to the same source data that powers their applications through license deals, partnerships, and programming interfaces. The guides that end up succeeding will be the ones who best weave together and manipulate that data into an extremely useful experience tied to a simple, elegant, and engaging user interface.

What makes each platform unique are their algorithms and user experience. At the end of the day, all have the same goal in helping people to find television shows to watch. But the best "algorithm" is actually one's friends, which is why social media will continue to grow as a trusted source for content discovery.

On September 22, 2011, Facebook announced a number of big changes to its platform at its annual F8 developer conference. Among the changes is an evolution of Facebook's "like" button to include other verbs such as "watch."[16] This represents a new level of focus around television show recommendations that leverages one's social graph to drive tune-in using trusted sources: your friends.

Does Advertising on Social TV Guides Make Sense for Brands?

When it first launched, 80 percent of TVGuide.com's advertising came from television networks through banners and page skins. Since the people who use social TV guides are primarily trying to find something to watch on TV, this is an extremely fertile ground for television programmers. As TVGuide.com's Christy Tanner explains:

> Television programmers' number one goal is to drive viewer tune-in, because ratings drive their business. There is no better place to advertise a television show than TVGuide.com. You can't go wrong with a really clear and simple tune-in ad. Those ads are to TVGuide.com users as fashion ads are to readers of *Vogue*; they're quasi content. People are coming to us to make decisions about what to watch on television, and an ad will help them to make that decision.

Forty-five percent of TVGuide.com's advertising now comes from nontelevision brands. The key, however, is to find ways of integrating one's brand into the natural behaviors of the user experience so that any advertising is optimally receptive to end-users. As fav.tv's Saverio Mondelli told us: "You hate seeing an ad that's not relevant to you. If we do step into that arena of putting ads on fav.tv, it's going to be done in a way that makes sense for the user and helps the user."

What brand advertisers should be keeping their eyes on is the data that is being produced from each of the program guides. Every profile created and every action taken creates a larger footprint by which to drive better TV show recommendations. That same data set can give brands the ability to hyper target at an individual user level based on that person's favorite TV shows and how they engage with them.

TAKE ACTION: SOCIAL TV GUIDES

Advertising opportunities within social TV guides are ripe for television networks promoting their shows. However, that does not mean that brands cannot play as well. The following are a few things to keep in mind as you plan your advertising on social TV guides:

1. *Know your audience.* The players within the social TV guide space each have a unique demographic make-up of users. So be sure to spend some time understanding the size and scale of each application's audience to ensure the best fit for your brand.
2. *Align versus intrude.* The social TV guide space has varying degrees of advertising opportunities—and some applications do not have any. Evaluate each one with an eye toward content alignment and integration of your brand message instead of blanketing available real estate with irrelevant juxtaposed ads.
3. *Plant some seeds.* People use social TV guides to find shows to watch. This is an opportunity to seed your advertising message adjacent to those shows where you also have a sizable broadcast presence. Doing so reinforces your brand association as individuals encounter it across multiple interrelated mediums.

Fasten Your Seatbelt; This Space Is Only Going to Change

By the time this book is published, the social TV guide landscape will look different. That is actually good news for your brand, since with time also comes a more thorough vetting of players and, of course, greater lessons on which to determine the best brand integration strategy.

Scan for More

Scan this QR code using your mobile device for videos and visuals of the examples and cases referenced throughout this chapter.

Don't have a smartphone with a QR reader app? No problem. You can access companion content directly by going to http://www .socialtvbook.net/tagged/chapter2.

3

TV Check-In Services

Creating Vertical Social Networks around Television

Nina Perez is a 37-year-old fiction writer living in Atlanta, Georgia. She is able to stay at home to help raise her two kids while working as a Web content specialist for an outdoor gear and apparel company. Working from home has an added benefit for Nina: She can get her job done on her laptop while simultaneously watching TV. Nina admits to being a television fanatic and says that the TV is literally on all day and in multiple rooms in the house (apparently she has four TiVos).

Nina had been using an iPhone application called GetGlue that allowed her to "check-in" to the TV shows she watched and earn rewards (known as stickers) based on her activity. She noticed while on Facebook one day that one of her friends shared their TV check-in from another application called Miso. Though Nina had never heard of it before, she loved the idea of having the ability to check-in to a specific TV episode as opposed to the entire TV show.

Nina downloaded the app and quickly became hooked. She has since amassed over 100 Miso followers, checked-in to over 1000 television episodes, and earned more than 45 badges. Nina uses Miso to check in to just about every TV show she watches; she then auto posts every check-in to Twitter and Facebook. She absolutely loves the conversations that ensue when her friends see her check-ins and leave comments on Facebook or tweet her back. She also appreciates how seeing other people's check-ins has led her to discover new TV shows to watch about which she would not have otherwise known.

Nina has also continued to use GetGlue; however, she only checks-in to TV shows that offer stickers because she has been in a competition with her friends as to who can collect the most. She is intrigued by how the game's reward system compels her to tune in to TV shows as they air; if she doesn't, she loses out on earning the sticker.

Even Nina's husband has gotten into the TV check-in trend after his recent smartphone upgrade, and cannot wait to receive his first physical batch of earned GetGlue stickers in the mail. Nina is most proud of her rare "Golden Cylon" sticker that she earned on GetGlue by watching a lot of science fiction TV shows. However, she also cited a surprise badge she received on Miso called "Parents Behaving Badly." She has no idea how she earned it but attests that she *is* a good mom—despite all of her TV watching.

In fact, Nina addresses the less-than-favorable reputation that people who watch a lot of television tend to get. She admits that while watching TV used to be a much more isolated and solitary experience, social media has enabled coviewing—albeit virtual—on a mass scale. "It used to be that you were a loser if you stayed in on a Friday night, but now my friends and I have virtual TV dates," Nina says.

TV check-in services are yet another way that television is being taken out of the solitary home environment and made into a fun and competitive social TV experience.

Location-Based Check-Ins Gave Rise to the TV Check-In

What's cool about Foursquare is that you're sharing your location and being seen in all kinds of places. But checking into a lot of different TV implies you're a couch potato. So we need to answer the question: How do you make watching a lot of TV cool?
—Ryan Osborn, Director of Social Media at NBC News

Years ago, the way in which one "checked-in" to a television show was simply to turn on the TV and watch. The notion of using a mobile application to *literally* broadcast to your friends what you are watching simply did not exist.

Then the rise in popularity of location-based social networks—such as Foursquare and Gowalla—brought the trend of checking-in by using one's mobile phone to physical places into the mainstream. This behavior was further fueled by the growth in smartphone adoption, along with advances in mobile device technology.

Foursquare's concept is simple: when one arrives at a given destination, they launch the Foursquare application—which displays all of the various locations around them within a very close radius— on their smartphone. Thanks to their mobile phone's built-in GPS, their exact location is likely at the top of the list. After making their selection, the user can optionally leave a message and post their check-in to Twitter and/or Facebook. Clicking a large green button is all that is left to do in order to check in and alert that individual's friends as to their whereabouts.

The appeal of location-based social networks lies at a few different levels. Not only do they help to facilitate both planned and serendipitous meet ups, it is also fun to see who else is checked-in and what reviews (in the form of "tips") people have provided about the given location. The applications' native game mechanics induce a sense of competitive participation through earned points and unique badges. Additionally, users' loyalty to various locations is rewarded with discounts, deals, and other specials.

The location-based check-in phenomenon caught the attention of several entrepreneurs in late 2009 who were intent upon bringing a similar concept to the world of entertainment. So they did— and by mid-2010, the public saw the birth of three separate TV/entertainment check-in mobile applications.

GetGlue Sees Itself As a Vertical Social Network Around Entertainment

We're going deep as a stand-alone social network around entertainment, specifically in the realm of television. We want to create the delightful experience for the end-user to socialize with fans and friends around the television programs that they're currently already watching and augmenting that experience in some capacity—and that's our bet.

—Fraser Kelton, COO at GetGlue

GetGlue was founded in 2007 and launched its full-fledged destination website in October of 2009.[1] The company focused a little more on books, movies, and music rather than television in its early days; however, all of that soon changed.

By using principles of the semantic Web[2] to help interpret meaning and context from the data it collects over time, GetGlue provides its users with personalized entertainment suggestions. As part of creating a profile when first joining the social network, new users are presented with a library of TV shows and asked to "like" 10 of them. This action lays the foundation for GetGlue's recommendations engine. As users "like" more and more TV shows—as well as movies, sports, books, and games—over time, their suggestions become increasingly fine-tuned, and therefore more relevant to them.

However, providing these kinds of personalized suggestions was just the beginning of GetGlue's story. It was not until the company released its iPhone app in June of 2010 (and in an iPad version three months later) that it truly began to take off.[3] By bringing utility, convenience, and simplicity to GetGlue through the power of mobile, the app introduced the idea of "checking in" to TV shows and other entertainment. GetGlue greatly reduced the barriers to engage on its platform by doing so.

The application's welcome screen presents users with six buttons—each of which represents an entertainment media type—in response to a simple prompt, "You are . . ." For example, one of the choices is "Watching TV." Clicking that button lists all of the TV shows that are currently trending as measured by each of their relative amount of recent GetGlue activity. If users cannot find the show within the trending list, they can use a search box at the top of the screen that is available. Clicking a show name reveals a large green "Check-In" button accompanied by other information about the show, including the app's built-in form of social currency: GetGlue stickers.

By incorporating a layer of game mechanics, GetGlue incentivizes engagement by rewarding its users with branded stickers that they can earn through predefined check-in parameters. Through over fifty partnerships with television networks and other entertainment companies, there are close to 3,000 available stickers up for grabs.[4] Upon earning 20 of these in their virtual form, they allow a user to unlock the ability to request the actual physical stickers from GetGlue, who mails them at no charge to the user.

On September 29, 2011, GetGlue announced a partnership with DirectTV that deeply embedded its check-in and community functionality into the pay TV provider's viewer interfaces.[5] By linking their GetGlue accounts, DirectTV subscribers are able to check-in to TV shows onscreen using the DirectTV remote as well as from the DirectTV iPad app. In addition to checking-in, DirectTV subscribers can pull up their GetGlue stream to see what their friends are watching and at the click of a button tune in to watch a given show themselves. This becomes a great way to discover new content, similar to the social TV guides that we illustrated in the previous chapter.

Social Impressions Give GetGlue Its Power

From the very first interaction at the point of sign-up, GetGlue encourages users to connect their Facebook and Twitter accounts so that they can easily share the TV shows to which they have checked in. Furthermore, GetGlue community members can follow each other, an option that lets others know about the actions they take via their respective activity feeds. All of this leads to new content discovery and increased probability for TV tune-in as social impressions are constantly being generated with each and every check-in.

There was an 800 percent increase in GetGlue check-ins over the course of six months, from January of 2011 to August of that same year.[6] Not only did August produce over 11 million check-ins for the month, but in June, the service averaged 100,000 check-ins shared to Facebook and Twitter per day. As a result, GetGlue estimated their average social impressions generated per day to be around 80 million.

The spike in engagement that GetGlue is experiencing is not just based on its user growth. The company has been working hard to bring richer entertainment partnerships to its user base—something that compels people to take action and participate.

True Blood Set a New Record for GetGlue

The fourth season premiere of HBO's cult vampire hit *True Blood* gave GetGlue a record number 38,000 check-ins (up from a mere 3,000 from its earlier season[7]). The previous single event GetGlue check-in record was set by the 2011 Oscars and amounted to 25 percent less check-ins.

To build anticipation toward the premiere, GetGlue ran a contest where fans could win a bottle of "Tru Blood" (carbonated beverage) by checking-in to the show and using the #TBWithdrawal hashtag. Not only would one receive a special *True Blood* sticker, they would also be entered into a daily drawing. In addition to the free drinks, winners would also receive an exclusive sticker. This helped to spur engagement by using competitive gamification techniques.

During the actual premiere—which aired on June 26, 2011—GetGlue unveiled a series of *True Blood* stickers, each of which corresponded to an upcoming episode.[8] Fans who checked in to all 12 episodes on GetGlue were entered into a drawing to win an item from the actual *True Blood* set.

What was particularly innovative about this partnership was that GetGlue's execution did not exist in a vacuum. Instead, it was tightly integrated into HBO Connect, which is the network's visualizer for the real-time backchannel. By utilizing cross-linking and promotion, GetGlue and HBO created a much more inclusive and complementary television viewing experience.

If GetGlue Really *Is* a Social Network, Is Facebook a Threat to Them?

GetGlue's COO Fraser Kelton explains the difference between a horizontal—and thus broad—social network like Facebook versus a vertical and deep one—which is the space in which GetGlue is playing. As Kelton explains:

> We've historically seen Facebook own the horizontal play connecting people to people. Is there room for a vertical social network connecting people through Television? The answer is very quickly becoming *yes*. The question that keeps coming up now is—will Facebook—or a strong horizontal like Google—'kill the vertical'? The answer we've historically seen is no. When Twitter emerged 24 to 36 months ago, people began asking the same questions. But Twitter went deep in the vertical, and their growth accelerated. Then the same thing happened with Foursquare and location-based platforms. Eighteen months ago, people were predicting that Facebook Places was going to kill Foursquare; but instead, it's accelerated their growth more than anything. We've seen that while the horizontal layer can add value and compete on some level, it usually can't go as deep as the vertical layer does.

We found a common theme throughout our interviews and across social TV topics—one that debates the merits of the "one size fits all solution" versus a niche solution that does a single thing really well. While the question is yet to be answered, there is no denying the growth rates and loyal fanatics that many of the niche players are currently enjoying.

Miso Aims Beyond the TV Check-In

In five years, there will be a second screen experience. We believe that there is a better way to watch TV and Miso is going to be part of it.
—Somrat Niyogi, Cofounder and CEO at Miso

Three months before GetGlue's iPhone app launched, Miso made its big debut, unveiling the concept of the TV check-in just in time for Austin's South by Southwest Interactive Festival in March of 2010. At the time, Miso positioned itself as the Foursquare of television, an analogy that the media and press immediately latched on to.[9]

Despite the number of apps available to help people decide what to watch on TV, the Google Ventures-backed company felt that a large gap existed—namely, one that made the experience of sharing television with friends *fun*. In its early days, Miso considered itself to be a "social entertainment game"; they emphasized gamification principles such as a points system and the ability to earn badges, which was reminiscent of the Foursquare app from which it drew some of its inspiration.

Inspiration Can Come When You Least Expect It

A funny thing happened to Miso cofounder Somrat Niyogi in early 2010: he surprisingly earned the "douchebag" badge one night while checking-in to Foursquare. This fueled Niyogi's desire to create Miso,[10] as that particular badge was not only difficult to earn—but (unsurprisingly) created a little controversy, given its name and implied meaning. Yet a lot of people were talking about it at the time, which only thrust Foursquare even more into the spotlight and helped to fuel its growth.

Niyogi took notice of the curious inquiries he spawned amongst the people within his own social graph as his newly earned badge was broadcast from his Facebook and Twitter accounts to his friends and followers. Coupled with the rise in mobile smartphone usage and the increased simplicity of social sharing, this experience was the inspiration that helped give birth to Miso.

The name "Miso" was chosen because of its short, sweet, and easy to spell wording. The founders hoped that it would take off via people's use of the term as a verb within the common lexicon—similar to the way that it has become normal to say, "Let me Google that" or "Facebook me." The company has grown its community into a base of over 250,000 engaged users who skew a bit male and fall within the 18 to 45 age demographic.

Miso Sets the Bar on User Experience

As Miso looks to build value for its community beyond the check-in, it is providing its users with companion opportunities to keep them engaged during the shows they are watching. The Miso app update that released on May 2, 2011 included a new "pick 'em" feature that poses a poll-like question about a given checked-in TV show. Miso participants are able to share their answer with their friends on the platform and through other social networks. Among the TV shows for which the feature was implemented includes the eighth season of *So You Think You Can Dance*.[11] Miso users could choose which dance contestant they felt was going to be voted off the show each week, and see how their choice ranked against the rest of the Miso community.

The Miso app's graphical user interface—available for the iPhone, iPad, and Android phones—is strikingly polished and intuitive to navigate. The "TV & Film" button at the center of the bottom navigation bar lists recently checked-in TV shows, followed by those that are trending. The trending shows also display the number of people who are currently checked-in.

The shows listed include a corresponding logo graphic, which makes it a lot faster—and more visually effective—to scan for them. Clicking a show brings up a synopsis page that provides a show description and list of cast members. A prominent "Pick An Episode" button details a program's recent episodes, followed by its past episodes grouped by season.

When a user selects an episode, they receive its description along with the cumulative rating the Miso community gave it. This allows users to check-in to specific TV shows and optionally rate them.

A "chatter" tab in the upper right corner displays comments and ratings that Miso community members are posting about the given TV show episode in real-time.

Miso Expands with the Help of Third-Party Developers

In May of 2011, Miso launched an app gallery showcasing third-party applications that had been built with its open application programming interface (API).[12] By leveraging the wider developer community, Miso is strategically accelerating its growth and innovation. As a result, the Miso app is now available for the Windows Phone 7 operating system. Another third-party-developed application synchs one's Miso friends with their Android phone contacts.

Miso hopes to find its way into many other platforms, devices, and experiences by opening up their code to ambitious programmers. The company and its app have jumped full force into the second screen synched content phenomenon—a topic that we address in the next chapter.

PHILO Enters the Market Thanks to a Rerun of *Animal House*

There are a bunch of reasons people check into TV shows. Game mechanics are real. This is not some kind of fad that's going away. It's kind of freakish, in a good way, how people really strive to have the most amount of points on their favorite TV shows.

—David Levy, CEO at PHILO

On a cold New York City evening in December of 2009, David Levy was watching a television rebroadcast of the classic movie *Animal House.* Levy was e-mailing back and forth with a buddy of his who was also tuning-in (but at his own house). As the two men discussed their real-time reactions, they reminisced back to a day when they originally saw the movie. And despite being in separate physical locations, they were still sharing the viewing experience. One of David's final e-mails sent to his friend that night posed the question, "Why can't we just check-in to TV?"

Shortly thereafter, the duo got to work designing a new iPhone application that was meant to connect people watching TV on a giant virtual sofa. In May of 2010, the application—PHILO, aptly named after the man credited with inventing television, Philo Farnsworth—launched just two months after Miso made its big debut. This made PHILO the second TV check-in application to hit the market; it would be joined by GetGlue's iPhone app one month later.

Shaquille O'Neal Starts Using PHILO

When TNT's *NBA Sprite Slam Dunk Contest* aired on February 19, 2011, a partnership with the network offered the PHILO community a virtual viewing party for those who checked-in using the app. Participants earned a "Slam Dunk badge" and were able to connect in real-time with Shaquille O'Neal, who was courtside giving a live play-by-play on PHILO.[13]

Shaq—who has a colossal social media following—awarded three PHILO users whom he deemed made the best comments a pair of his size 23 sneakers. PHILO reported that viewing parties like this typically generate over one million Facebook social impressions from users who share their interactions during programs.[14]

PHILO Gets Acquired and Sunsets Its Check-In App

In late April of 2011, David and his team strategically paused for a moment to take a step back. They discussed where PHILO was headed amidst a crowd of seemingly similar TV check-in apps—including new players like IntoNow—that had arose in the space. The increasingly crowded market prompted the company to start deemphasizing the TV check-in application it had been supporting for about a year. Instead, David and his team reallocated PHILO's resources toward a new effort that helped TV networks and brands target audiences based on an aggregated set of TV check-in data.

This move set the stage for check-in search engine LocalResponse to acquire PHILO on August 4, 2011. While LocalResponse—where David now serves as an advisor[15]—had already been providing brands with the ability to target tweets to individuals using location-based check-in data, integrating PHILO would expand their business model to include TV check-ins.

IntoNow Puts a New Spin on the TV Check-In

We view ourselves as a companion product to TV that helps surface all of the social elements that are there already. We're just providing a platform for people to be able to easily do that.

—Adam Cahan, CEO at IntoNow

One appealing feature of consumer tech company IntoNow is the one-click TV check-in capability that it provides to users. Using patented audio fingerprinting technology, the app tracks what a user watches on television and automatically "tags" the show (the equivalent of checking-in). IntoNow—which launched on January 31, 2011—was quickly dubbed as the "Shazam for TV."[16]

Because the company indexed 130 television channels representing over 2.5 million broadcast airings, IntoNow set itself apart from its competition out of the gate. However, CEO Adam Cahan warns against the dangers of putting IntoNow—or other startups like them—into a vertical category. "You have to be careful about who you define as your competition, especially as an early stage company. When you determine who that competitive set is, you start to emulate them."

In April of 2011, a new version of the app gave IntoNow's 500,000 users at the time new features that focused on the post check-in experience. The upgraded functionality allowed IntoNow users to have in-app TV show discussions and receive content recommendations from friends.[17]

Yet certain features were glaringly missing from both the original and upgraded application; specifically, the badges and points systems that were now typical to the location and entertainment check-in categories. IntoNow felt strongly that making connections within the application and engaging with relevant content was what would drive repeat usage behavior—without the need for game mechanics.[18]

Yahoo! Buys IntoNow and Secures a Deal with *Project Runway*

On the morning of April 25, 2011—just three months after IntoNow's launch[19]—news broke about Yahoo!'s acquisition of the company. At that point, the app's users were generating over 35,000 tags per day. While some felt the sale was extremely premature,[20] IntoNow was thrilled to have their seven-person team all join Yahoo! and enjoy the benefit of a full sales force to help drive media partnerships.

In July of 2011, Yahoo! announced IntoNow's integration with season nine of Lifetime Television's hit program *Project Runway*. Fresh out of the gate with a brand new Android version and over one million users already on its iPhone app, the product enticed *Project Runway* fans with exclusive content in exchange for tagging TV episodes. IntoNow made it incredibly easy for viewers to engage while watching the show. By simply clicking the application's big green button (demarked with a TV icon), guests were able to unlock upcoming episode sneak peeks, photos, and guest judge bios. IntoNow users could also partake in *Project Runway*-related polls, and enter contests.[21]

There Is Something in a Name

One might notice upon looking closely at IntoNow's logo that a "fill in the blank" space separates the two words that comprise the product's name. It was born of the notion of how people, when conversing about television, often say, "I'm really into (*show name*) now."

Designing the application around the strengths of the specific devices on which it runs not only makes its user experience incredibly simple, it also essentially guarantees that the product will continue to evolve in ways that are almost impossible to predict at this stage. In the meantime, IntoNow continues to grow its user base and device footprint and select the kind of partnerships that complement the application's user experience.

We Check-In Because We Are Wired to Share

TV Guide asked people why they share what they are watching on television within social networks, and 77 percent cited the desire to tell their friends what shows they like as their top reason.[22] There is a certain level of personal endorsement we make when we check-in to a show—which may be one reason why our sharing behaviors vary by gender.

A data analysis study conducted by GetGlue in July of 2011 found a higher percentage of women checking-in to episodic television shows, despite the fact that its user base is pretty equally spread across males and females.[23] Their theory for the discrepancy is that men are embarrassed to check-in to TV shows they deem to be "feminine" (but that they watch nonetheless). GetGlue does not see the reverse of this behavior when it comes to their female user base. The question, then, becomes: at what point in time are people checking-in to their favorite TV shows?

Miso confirmed that most TV check-ins take place at the very start of a show.[24] The company analyzed and compared check-in data for the 2011 Super Bowl, Oscars, and Grammy Awards and plotted the results on a line graph. The graph showed huge spikes at the beginning of each of the shows followed by a gradual tapering of check-ins as the show progressed. Unsurprisingly, the data displayed several similarities to location-based check-ins, as most people check-in upon arrival at a given destination.

To add a little more color to its raw check-in data, Miso layered on the results of a user survey it conducted in March of 2011. Fifty-one percent of the respondents said they check in before or at the beginning of a TV show. Twenty-seven percent delay their check-in to a point during the show; in many cases, they wait until something "interesting" happens that compels them to want to broadcast a comment about it.

As we discussed in Chapter 1, television viewers do not just comment about TV programs, but TV advertising as well. It was therefore just a matter of time until mobile devices would be used to engage with ads on television and deliver users with some kind of offer or exclusive content in return. [25]

The Check-In Phenomenon Hits TV Commercials

If you tag a commercial and an MP3 shows up in your device, that's pretty cool. You just transcended two different screens and gave me as a user a very personal experience. That's the kind of magic that we're after, and want to provide in big, scaleable ways.
—Adam Cahan, CEO at IntoNow

Just before its sale to Yahoo!, IntoNow partnered with Pepsi as part of Pepsi MAX's Major League Baseball sponsorship and produced a television commercial featuring various MLB legends. The first 50,000 IntoNow users who found and tagged it unlocked a mobile coupon to receive a free bottle of Pepsi MAX redeemable at select retail stores.

According to IntoNow CEO Adam Cahan, this was the first time anyone had been able to generate a unique coupon within a mobile device. What also made the execution of the brand integration stand out is that IntoNow was able to, in effect, bridge the digital and physical worlds using mobile in a very simple, useful, and elegant way.

However, Cahan cautions about dialing up advertising within the IntoNow platform too quickly, and explains that "We actually turn down advertising. We often are approached with a standard request to put banners in the app. But we're still looking for ways for advertising to coexist with our product and for the two to actually add value to one another."

This is yet another echo of a common theme we heard from many of these organizations' leaders: the need for advertising to be applied in such a way so that it complements the unique user experience of the environment.

Shazam Brings Its Built-In User Base to TV

For years, people have been Shazaming TV shows and ads for the music featured, so it was a logical next step for people to Shazam them for the shows and ads, themselves. And, because the tag lives on in their tag list, they can interact with the program or brand in their own time, "snacking" on the media when they're in line, waiting for the bus, or just have a couple of minutes to spare.
                        —David Jones, EVP of Marketing at Shazam

Originally known for its ability to recognize music, Shazam is the fourth most downloaded mobile application of all time. It has exceeded 150 million users and is growing at over a million more per week. "Shazamers"—as the company calls its users—are currently tagging over four million songs per day.

Shazam works by matching a short captured sample of music against its database using audio fingerprinting. If this sounds like the product might have copied IntoNow, think again—Shazam has been around since 1999. They released their iPhone app on July 10 2008,[26] nearly three years before IntoNow launched its app for television.

The first time Shazam integrated with a TV commercial was for a Dockers ad that debuted during Super Bowl XLIV on February 7, 2010.[27] When initiated, the Shazam app recognized the Dockers commercial as it aired, and unlocked additional complementary content. While this integration got a good amount of buzz, what seemed to put Shazam officially on the TV map was Old Navy's spring advertising campaign announced on February 17, 2011.[28]

The TV spots featured original "Old Navy Records" music videos and included an animated Shazam "bug" in the lower right-hand corner. Shazaming the commercial presented the user with several options including a page that featured the Old Navy fashions from the music video. Users also had the opportunity to download the song for free. According to Shazam, one of the Old Navy TV spots was in the top three most tagged songs for the week; it even beat out extraordinarily popular singer Lady Gaga. And 27 percent of the people who ended up Shazaming the Old Navy commercials went to the Old Navy mobile storefront to shop for the featured looks.

There is an addictive instant gratification that comes from using apps like Shazam and IntoNow. While IntoNow started off with TV shows and is making their way into TV commercials, Shazam did just the opposite. On January 20, 2011—eleven months after their Dockers TV advertising integration—Shazam announced a partnership with cable channel SyFy.[29] Users who Shazamed episodes of the program *Being Human* gained access to exclusive preview videos, music playlists, and contest entries.

Shazam continued to grow into television. News broke in June of 2011 that the company had raised $32 million in venture capital specifically earmarked to expand its TV offering.[30] The company added USA Network, HBO, and Bravo to its roster of TV program integrations.

The CW Partners with Shopkick

Shopkick's location-based iPhone app, which gives you offers and rewards for simply walking into a store, launched on August 17, 2010 coupled to a deep partnership with BestBuy.[31] The application's users are automatically checked-in to select retail stores when they walk through the doors. Shopkick does this by listening for a specific audio tone (inaudible to humans) that is emitted by a physical speaker at the entrance of participating retailers.

Simply by walking into a store, a Shopkick users earns "kicks" (the app's form of virtual currency) that can accumulate with additional in-store app engagement. Users can redeem their kicks for partner retailer gift cards or a growing list of other rewards—including iTunes gift cards, movie tickets, and Facebook credits. Users can also donate their kicks to various nonprofit causes.[32]

With over two million users, Shopkick has grown its retail partnerships to include select Macy's, Target, Sports Authority, and Crate & Barrel locations, among several others. While the application can be used at any retail store, larger amounts of kicks are earned at those who have partnered with Shopkick directly.

The slightly skewed female user base—with close to 50 percent between the ages of 25 and 39 years old—produced 100 million check-ins during Shopkick's first six months.[33] These early successes and extremely strong growth compelled the company to turn its attention to TV.

The idea of closing the loop from the person sitting on the couch watching a television commercial to their entry and engagement in-store brought Shopkick and television network The CW together for an exclusive partnership. During the fall 2011 television season, advertisers had the opportunity to Shopkick-enable their TV commercial and offer special deals, instant coupons, or other rewards to viewers of The CW for the first time.

What differentiated this execution from those involving Shazam is that The CW would display lower thirds during the actual TV show itself—just before a commercial break occurred—to alert viewers to launch their Shopkick app. This was incredibly fruitful advertising for Shopkick, and simultaneously provided an additional hook for The CW viewers to tune in to their favorite shows live.

The May 19, 2011 issue of the *New York Times* quotes Shopkick CEO Cyriac Roeding as saying, "The cell phone is the only interactive medium that you carry with you while you're watching TV *and* shopping in store, and is therefore the only interactive medium that can function as the bridge between the TV screen and the store shelf."[34]

The advertiser, of course, is the big winner here; they are enabled with the means to help measure the relationship of TV spot tune-in with in-store traffic (albeit with an incentive involved). But the idea of brand integrations and couponing has not just been limited to the newer TV check-in players.

The Original TV Check-In Apps Get into the Ad Business Too

On January 9, 2011, animated television sitcom *Bob's Burgers* premiered on Fox. Through a three-pronged partnership, GetGlue users who checked-in to the new animated comedy while watching it live earned two exclusive stickers. The first was a *Bob's Burgers* show sticker, and the second was a sticker from national restaurant chain Fatburger that doubled as a scannable mobile coupon for a free medium burger.[35]

In another instance, GetGlue users who checked-in to the July 12, 2011 *MLB All-Star Game* were welcomed by two stickers—one of which was MLB and Fox branded.[36] The other sticker was for *X Factor* and provided a teaser tie-in with the game. This sticker included a prominently placed Pepsi logo as part of the brand's sponsorship of the show. In effect, the sticker acted as a banner ad for Pepsi that came with built-in receptivity and longevity—since GetGlue stickers are coveted keepsakes for many users.

And on September 15, 2011, GetGlue announced a one-month partnership with *Entertainment Weekly* and Gap for the fall TV season. Users who checked-in, week after week, to premieres of new television series appearing on *Entertainment Weekly*'s "list of great shows" (like *New Girl*, *Pan Am*, and *The X Factor*) would unlock exclusive stickers accompanied by a 40 percent discount on purchases at participating Gap stores.[37] Gap shoppers simply needed to mention the discount redemption code from their unlocked sticker at the register upon check-out. Within the first week of the partnership, over 75,000 people unlocked the special, according to GetGlue.

While the advertising executions so far have been intelligently integrated within their individual partnerships for the most part, the question remains as to whether or not TV viewers will want to switch between (and in some cases download) several apps in order to get check-in offers on various commercials using different platforms. Since none of these apps has yet emerged as the de facto standard, it is very possible that we will encounter a scenario where a TV show one is watching has, for instance, a GetGlue brand tie-in and at least one other commercial over the course of the broadcast that is Shazam or IntoNow-enabled.

The TV Check-In Space Has Become Crowded

There are new TV check-in apps that continue to emerge, and several others that we did not cover in this chapter. Tunerfish has been around since late 2010 and upgraded its iPhone check-in application in July of 2011. TVtak is an app that checks its users into TV shows just by taking a picture of them. WiO was born using a similar audio detection model reminiscent of Shazam and IntoNow. Even *TV Guide* has an "I'll Watch" check-in feature that was being used about 20,000 times per day toward the end of the 2011 spring TV season[38] and 40,000 times per day come fall premiere week of that same year.

The irony is that most if not all of the applications in this space do not call themselves TV check-in apps. GetGlue identifies itself as a vertical social network, Miso touts itself as a second screen platform, and so on. Checking-in (or its equivalent) is a mere starting point—a doorway into other content and features.

We have found that while most of these applications still have a comparatively small (but growing) user base, it is their hooks into larger social networks like Facebook and Twitter that give them broader reach and appeal. Sharing one's check-in to Facebook, for instance, often is a catalyst for further social engagement. Just because that engagement moved from the check-in app where it initiated to another platform does not necessarily make it any less valuable. In fact, the social impressions it spawns actually amplifies its worth in many cases.

TAKE ACTION: TV CHECK-IN SERVICES

The TV check-in space is evolving at breakneck speed. There are many players that seem similar on the surface, but each have a unique offering. Here are a few considerations as you evaluate a suitable match and use case for your brand.

1. *Get to know the users.* Not all check-in applications are created equal. It is important to look not only at the audience size and demographics, but also how quickly it is growing, how active the user base is, and to what degree they create social impressions. This will start to give you a sense of the application's vitality and reach potential.

2. *Think cross-channel.* Individual yet related channel media experiences work better when they are blended together. If your brand is already planning a notable TV series sponsorship or integration—and that series has also partnered with a TV check-in service—look to connect media channels by embedding your brand through a sponsorship with the given check-in service to provide an additional layer of brand engagement that reinforces your television media buy.

3. *Color outside the lines.* With emergence of new tools comes increased opportunities for innovation. Every one of the TV check-in companies is continuously experimenting with new features to see what sticks. The receptivity of these companies is very high

(continued)

> *(continued)*
>
> to explore custom branded partnerships to design a unique and ownable branded experience. Ensure your content and its related calls-to-action include a compelling "hook" where users want to engage with and share your brand.

It's Not Just About the Check-In

It is easy for some people to put their "focus group-of-one" hat on and dismiss the TV check-in space. You may be one of those people. However, it is important to keep in mind that while you may not engage with these platforms yourself, there are a sizable and, in many cases, growing number of people who are. And it is almost a guarantee that this includes members of your target audience. The "check-in" is simply the entry-point into something more. And it is how you define the "more" that will determine your brand's success in this space.

Scan for More

Scan this QR code using your mobile device for videos and visuals of the examples and cases referenced throughout this chapter.

Don't have a smartphone with a QR reader app? No problem. You can access companion content directly by going to http://www .socialtvbook.net/tagged/chapter3.

The Second Screen

Enhancing TV with Synched Content Experiences

Olen Weaver, age 37, started his career in his home state of Oklahoma as a sound engineer designing audio systems for major concerts across the country for over 19 years. After his son was born, Olen wanted to make sure he stayed close to home; so he turned another one of his passions, photography, into a full-fledged local business. When shooting photos as a hobby, Olen uses his Nikon D300 to photograph picturesque landscapes inspired by his childhood obsession for *National Geographic*. In contrast, his professional studio focuses on capturing *people* through portraits as well as candid moments from weddings and other events.

In June of 2010, Olen purchased an iPad despite his trepidation as to how useful a device it would be for him. Today, he cannot imagine life without it. His beloved tablet has become embedded in every aspect of his business, from invoicing and client bookings to sound level measurements and portfolio showcasing.

One day, while using The Weather Channel app to check his local forecast, Olen saw an advertisement for a new TWC show called *From the Edge with Peter Lik*. After watching a few preview video clips online, Olen became hooked on wanting to see more from the world-famous photographer and immediately set his DVR to record the TV series. Along the way, he discovered that The Weather Channel was also offering a free iPad app to act as a real-time synchronized "second screen" companion to the television broadcast. He immediately downloaded the app and has since watched every episode of *From the Edge* as a two-screen experience. He views the main programming from his big screen television, which is complemented by extra content that gets pushed out to him on his iPad.

Given his background in sound design, Olen appreciates how the *From the Edge* app uses the iPad's built-in microphone to detect audio from the television broadcast and delivers exclusive content that is timed with specific in-show events. He remembers one particular episode where Peter Lik travelled to Yosemite National Park. Although there was a little bit of interaction with the park ranger during the TV broadcast, the iPad app delivered a much more in-depth human interest back story as to how he came to develop a lifelong love for Yosemite.

Another feature that Olen really likes are the interactive polls that appear during key moments of the on-air broadcast, which often showcase a choice of photos that Peter Lik captured during the episode, and ask the audience to vote for their favorite. The instant gratification that Olen gets from seeing the combined results from the second screen app's user community adds a compelling dimension to his overall television experience. While he mentioned that many television networks may post extra content for their TV shows on their websites or Facebook pages, he is not apt to go hunt it down. Instead, Olen loves the way in which content comes to him through his iPad as an extension of his television set.

Even though *From the Edge* is his first experience using a second screen companion app, Olen believes this is the future of television, as social media is a growing and powerful force that connects TV audiences and allows them to interact directly with the show *and* each other.

Welcome to a Multiscreen Television Experience

For decades, the ecosystem of TV was simply the familiar television set: a box with only one screen that displayed video and graphics accompanied by sound. Whereas people used to just watch television, nowadays, they *experience* it. Evolving technology and human behavior have given birth to television's second screen, adding a parallel and synchronized layer of interactive companion content to the TV experience.

It all started with the laptop; specifically, when Nielsen reported back in 2010 that 60 percent of Americans use the Internet simultaneously while watching television.[1] Networks began to examine potential ways to capitalize on this behavior as a complement to watching a TV broadcast. In Chapter 1, we highlighted the MTV Video Music Awards' visualized backchannel and the 2010 Emmy Awards' backstage live streaming as two specific tactics that television networks utilized to produce synchronized second screen experiences for their viewers.

The rise in smartphone and tablet devices has additionally brought what many refer to as the "third and fourth" screens to TV. Though we hinted at mobile second screen experiences in the previous chapter, that was just the tip of the iceberg. The accessibility and interoperability of mobile has opened up a whole new range of companion television possibilities.

To keep things simple, the phrase "the second screen" as used throughout this chapter will encompass all companion television screen devices including laptops, smartphones, and tablets.

It May Seem That the Second Screen Is TV's Enemy

We know through all of our research that more and more people watch TV with another device near them. And as the world has migrated from desktops to laptops, that has changed more. As we migrate from laptops to tablets, it will take place even more frequently. You have to fight for people's attention and hope that they're interacting with your content while they're watching TV— not somebody else's.

—Julie DeTraglia, SVP, Strategic Digital and Broadcast Marketing Research at NBC

In May of 2011, video ad network YuMe published the results of a video "Distraction Study" it had conducted with the help of Interpublic Group (IPG).[2] YuMe and IPG were hoping to learn more about the top behaviors that pull one's attention away from watching TV (and online video) ads. They were also researching the degree of ad avoidance that occurs beyond active DVR ad skipping, based on their calculations (using data from Magna Global) that only 2 percent of all TV spots are DVR skipped.[3]

The study took place on March 15 and 16, 2011 at the IPG Media Lab in Los Angeles. Forty-eight local individuals, who were recruited to watch television for an hour, were chosen through a survey that screened candidates who watch both TV *and* online video. Fifty-two percent of the participants were male, 48 were female, and over half were employed full-time. Only 23 percent of the sample had children under 18.

Participants in the sample, who were pretty evenly distributed across an 18- to 69-year-old age bracket, were asked to bring in any supplemental items (a.k.a., "distraction media") that would best re-create their particular TV viewing experience. In addition to some obvious diversions, one individual brought his electric guitar.

Upon arriving at the lab, participants were outfitted with a biometric bracelet that measured their temperature, stress, and "emotional condition." As they watched TV using a DVR (that happened to be loaded with their favorite shows), three cameras recorded their every move. A facial tracking algorithm measured "intellectual engagement" by synching a subject's eyes when viewing the TV screen with the exact time stamped content they were watching. This was then correlated to when and by what they became distracted.

YuMe and IPG found the biggest source of TV viewer distraction to be the mobile phone. Over 60 percent of their sample looked away from the TV screen to use their phone; not necessarily to make or answer calls, but to browse the Web, text, and check e-mail. Thirty-three percent were distracted by a laptop. The study's findings report summed this up by saying, "Smartphones are a persistent companion to video content."

The key word here is "companion"—meaning "in addition to," not "a replacement of." Mobile certainly is not television's enemy; it is instead an opportunity for broadcast networks, cable companies, equipment manufacturers, app developers, and advertisers to enhance the TV experience by connecting one medium to another.

Mobile and TV Are Like Two Peas in a Pod

Though there's been so much money and effort invested in interactive TV over the past 10 to 15 years, it's never been able to scale. Smartphones and tablets have come into the picture, thereby enabling an entirely new world of interactive TV that we call the second screen. Taking an easy-to-use mobile device and tying it to the television unlocks a tremendous amount of potential.
— Cory Bergman, Founder of *Lost Remote*

In July of 2011, Cory Bergman of popular social TV blog *Lost Remote* made the case for the mobile second screen experience. He cited a report from rich media ad network, MediaMind, on mobile advertising that included insights as to what time of day mobile users click the most on ads—which happened to be during prime-time television hours.[4] Mobile usage is at its heaviest between 7 to 9 PM. The question then becomes: are these individuals in front of the television *while* they are on their mobile devices?

In early 2011, Yahoo partnered with Nielsen to interview over 8,000 Americans between the ages of 13 and 64 years old. They found that 86 percent of the group used mobile while watching TV, and 24 percent of that group browsed content related to the television show they were watching. Twenty-three percent use their device to get more information about a TV spot they saw.[5]

While tablet penetration is still only in the single digits,[6] Nielsen reported in May of 2011 that the place where people use their tablet device (i.e., iPad) most frequently is in front of the television.[7] A survey of 12,000 Internet-connected device owners revealed that 70 percent claim to use their tablet while watching TV. And 30 percent of the time they spend on the device is in front of the television—which represents the tablet's top situational activity (using it in bed was second at only 21 percent).[8]

Second Screen Applications Push Related Content Directly to You ━━━━━━━

There's a better way to get information about a TV show. Right now, people go to Google and type something. We did a survey of about 7,000 of our users and found that only five percent of people go directly to a TV network's website to go get information. And, by the way, there's tons of good stuff there. Instead, they skip the network site and go to places like Wikipedia or IMDB.

—Somrat Niyogi, CEO at Miso

The springboard that propelled the idea of second screen applications as a companion for TV is based on a simple principle: we are naturally curious human beings who are compelled to feed that curiosity. Since most of us have some form of an Internet-connected second screen handy while watching TV, we have instant access to seemingly boundless information about a show as a means to help gratify our inherent curiosity.

Think about the number of times you go online to search for information related to a TV show you are watching. What is it that motivates you to do so? Perhaps you just started tuning in to a series and want to learn more about the show itself, such as how many seasons it has been on, episode synopses, and any back story. Another popular trigger is that you either recognize one of the show's actors or want to seek out more information about him or her. Perhaps you think they are attractive, and are curious about how old and tall they really are, where they were born, whether or not they are married, and any other gossip about them.

Instead of making the TV viewer constantly play Sherlock Holmes by having to search, filter, and mine through data to uncover the information they seek, applications on the second screen can, in theory, deliver relevant companion content directly to viewers during pertinent times as they watch TV. The potential to create resonant television experiences across screens is limitless. Finding the sweet spot where form, function, and content appeal to the masses, however, is the Holy Grail for second screen success—and the nut has not quite yet been cracked.

The challenge that application developers must overcome is that not every user wants the exact same information at the exact same time at the exact same frequency as every other user of the app. While there are some commonalities, second screen experiences are not ubiquitous—a situation that causes TV networks and tech companies to maintain a test and learn philosophy while trying to solve for many competing variables and behaviors.

Television Coviewing Apps Come in Many Flavors

Since 2010, TV networks have produced a barrage of coviewing apps that are predominantly centered on televison's prime second screen device: the iPad. We have categorized these apps into three main buckets.

Viewers can download *series*-specific apps for a particular show and use them over the course of the series' run. *Event*-specific apps are typically downloaded and used once or very infrequently for major tentpole television broadcasts, such as awards shows. *Network*-specific apps work across a set of shows for a given television network, thereby providing companion content for particular TV series without the need to download multiple applications.

The benefit of the last category is clear: a network need only convert a tablet user to download their application once, thereby eliminating one of the barriers to future usage on other shows within the given network. On the other hand, the argument in favor of offering series-specific applications is that TV viewers generally identify with a television show's—not *network's*—brand. By having a much more customized (versus templatized) second screen experience for a given show, the companion content can be that much more unique and, arguably, compelling. But it often comes at the expense of higher development and maintenance costs.

The universe of companion iPad applications provides many other ways to further differentiate the various uses for these features. For instance, the series-specific category gives networks the opportunity to design apps for scripted shows, reality TV, sports, or news—giving each one different nuances from a content-and-features perspective.

The technology used to power the apps is another way to categorize them. Some of the current companion iPad applications use audio fingerprinting or watermark technology (explained in the last chapter) to truly synchronize what one is watching with the exact moment during which companion content is pushed out. In this case, users will have a consistent and repeatable second screen companion experience— whether or not the show is watched live, on demand, or via DVR.

Other apps opt not to employ any audio synching technology, and instead promote live tune-in by simply releasing companion content to application users during a given TV show's original airtime. Using this method can create a user experience that feels somewhat similar to the audio synched apps, presuming the user is watching live.

Regardless of the application's flavor, its intent is to provide television viewers with an enhanced content experience that drives tune-in, loyalty, and sharing—and offers advertisers another place to reach and engage with their target audience.

The First Broadcast-to-Tablet Synchronized Apps Appeared in 2010

ABC's short-lived *My Generation* premiered on September 23, 2010. The "mockumentary" style show followed the lives of nine students during their senior year at fictional Roosevelt High School in Austin, Texas. Set in the year 2000, the group was comprised of the conventional high school archetypes: the jock, the beauty queen, the overachiever, the punk, the wallflower, the nerd, the brain, the rich kid, and, of course, the rock star.

The show's plot twist came when the same film crew caught up with the former students 10 years after their graduation to see how their lives turned out. The series was a constant switch between the past and present and compared the former high school students' hopes, dreams, and ambitions to the realities and unexpected turns of life.

As part of the fall premiere, ABC promoted its *My Generation* companion iPad app, which garnered quite a lot of buzz. As the first of its kind, it used Nielsen's brand new Media-Sync technology to listen for audio watermarks within the broadcast in order to synchronize the first screen (the TV) with the content served on the second screen (the iPad).[9] Nielsen's Media-Sync platform works similarly to Shazam and IntoNow's respective audio fingerprinting technology, both of which were featured in the previous chapter.

Launching the app revealed a stunning and clean user interface with a big red button on the bottom right of the screen prompting users to "Sync with Show."[10] Clicking this button initiated the Media-Sync routine at any point during the live or time-shifted broadcast. As the iPad's built-in microphone captured a sample of the TV broadcast to create a position match, the ABC logo slid down on the second screen display to expose a moving audio-wave "listening . . ." indicator. After several seconds, a message appeared in place of the synching indicator saying: "You are now synched with this episode of *My Generation*. Stay tuned to get bonus info, trivia, polls, and more during the show!"

And that is exactly what happened—the first of the content extras was pushed out during the show's opening credits, introducing the viewing audience to the Roosevelt High School seniors. A poll appeared asking, "What were you like in high school?" and listed the various stereotypes as possible answers. An indicator in the lower left-hand portion of the screen counted down the remaining time users had to lock in their answers. Choosing an answer—for instance, "The Overachiever"—revealed how one's response stacked up against all of the other users' responses as a percentage.

In order to avoid iPad users having to keep looking away from the TV screen, wondering if another piece of companion content was pushed to the second screen, a nonintrusive audio notification served as an alert. As new content appeared, old content moved down on the screen. One could easily use the iPad's swipe feature to scroll and review all previous content that was, essentially, a stack of discrete modules.

Unfortunately, *My Generation's* low ratings caused the TV series to be cancelled after just two broadcast airings—a reminder to all that technology alone is not able to draw mass television viewership. An audience's anchor always starts with resonant content. While the second screen experience may be compelling, it is, after all, still just the *second* screen. However, all was not lost, as ABC went on to use the *My Generation* iPad app's design, learnings, and architecture to create a similar companion application for season eight of *Grey's Anatomy* in 2011.[11]

Are Scripted Dramas Lean-Forward Experiences?

People approach different TV shows in different ways; it's a much richer spectrum than lean-forward lean-back.
   —Robin Sloan, Content and Programming at Twitter

My Generation and *Grey's Anatomy* are both scripted dramas and therefore, arguably, a much more immersive television viewing experience. It was interesting that the third major series-specific iPad companion app deployed was also a drama: Fox's *Bones*. The app launched on February 10, 2011, midway through the program's sixth season. However, one significant difference between ABC's and Fox's app is that Fox does not employ Nielsen's Media-Sync technology. They instead gather time zone information from the user's iPad during live viewing and cascade content based on the clock versus a true synch to broadcast execution using audio cues.[12]

Those who choose to watch a given *Bones* episode time-shifted versus live can press a button when the show begins which tells the app to start the clock and pace out the companion content based on predetermined time intervals. In addition, Fox embeds the social media backchannel directly into the iPad app, and provides a list of songs from each given episode's soundtrack with direct links to download any of them on iTunes.[13]

Since it is still in the early days of this kind of technology, the question remains as to whether or not synched second screen experiences will attract mass audiences. ABC Vice-President of Digital Media Rick Mandler makes a very important point:

> When you're watching a scripted drama, you're transported into the magical world of that drama. And every time we ask you to interact, to pull out of that magical world and get into the real-world, it's not as nice or as much fun as it is in the magical world. And then you have to re-engage with the magical world, which is a huge cognitive load. To let go of a narrative to engage with something that's in the real-world and then pick the narrative thread back up again is asking a lot from a television viewer.

Therefore, it is not a question as to whether or not people will engage on the second screen during dramas; it is a question as to how many people will choose to do so. Then again, all dramas may not be created equal; for as Twitter's Robin Sloan purports, "What could be more immersive than an HBO show? It has an incredibly high production value and engrossing storyline; yet HBO is even celebrating the fact that people are tweeting the craziest, most demystifying moments from their shows."

The key for television networks during this nascent period for social TV is to continue to have an appetite for trial and error. And part of being open to this is to test across different types of shows and audiences—and being comfortable with the failure that produces productive learning and insights.

From Drama to Reality, the Second Screen Expands Its Horizons

The third companion app to employ Nielsen's Media-Sync platform is The Weather Channel's first foray into original programming with its TV series entitled *From the Edge with Peter Lik*,[14] hosted by the well-known Australian photographer. The show, which premiered on March 31, 2011, chronicles Peter's journey across the United States as he searches for the most "dramatic landscapes."[15]

You may wonder what the show's tie is to The Weather Channel. Peter has to brave the weather as he travels from one place to another—which is severe at times. The 13-episode series seems ripe for a second screen companion experience, especially when compared to a scripted drama. There is a natural inclination to want to learn more about the locations featured in the series as well as interact with the photographs that Peter captures.

And that is exactly what differentiates the *From the Edge with Peter Lik* iPad app from the others in its category. Yes, it has the synchronized polls and quiz formats architecturally similar to its second screen brethren; however, it also provides pertinent behind-the-scenes footage as well as close-ups of the many photos taken within each episode. Since the show is based on Peter's photography, it is a great way to use the second screen to bring these photos to a more tangible life. The TV screen tells the story about how the photos are taken, and the second screen literally puts them into viewers' hands.

The Second Screen Enables Sports Fans to Play Along

Certain kinds of programming are going to be conducive to a second screen experience and some will absolutely not be. Sports represents a massive opportunity whereas the nature of the interaction is such that people will want more information at junctures that are appropriate. Sports are not like dramas; there's a lot of downtime—time

*that could be used to review statistics or additional information
which is hugely of interest to sports fans.*
                        — Andrew Wallenstein, TV Editor at *Variety*

While we could write a whole other book about social media's
impact on the sports industry, we would be remiss if we failed to give
a brief nod to the innovation that is taking place on the second screen
while watching televised games. Major League Baseball's *At Bat*
companion app—available across smartphone and tablet devices—
gives users real-time stats, player cards, and video highlights.[16]

Baseball is not the only sports genre to exploit the second screen.
The 2011 NBA playoffs gave fans access to the free *NBA Game Time*
iPad app[17] that interactively displayed information about on-court
players, scoring percentages, and a visual mapping of made and
missed shots—all in real-time.[18]

While MLB's companion solution supports the entire season
(similar to a TV series), NBA's iPad app falls into our event-specific
category of second screen applications joined by other tentpole
events such as awards shows, ceremonies, and miniseries.

The Kennedys Miniseries Turns the Second Screen into a Giant History Lesson

After a bit of content controversy, *The Kennedys* finally made its television debut on April 3, 2011, when it landed itself on ReelzChannel.
As the title suggests, the eight-part miniseries depicts John F.
Kennedy's rise to the White House, his presidency, and his tragic
assassination.[19] Using flashbacks to tell a story within a story, viewers
see a portrayal of the Kennedy family beginnings with Joe Kennedy
Senior at the helm.

ReelzChannel offered viewers an iPad app to accompany the
series that creates an interesting juxtaposition between an acted-out
portrayal of events broadcast on the TV screen versus content from

corresponding actual events served on the second screen.[20] When users first launch the iPad app, a splash page featuring the main characters of Bobby Kennedy, Joe Kennedy Senior, Jackie Kennedy, and JFK displays a prominent "JOIN THE CONVERSATION" call-to-action. Upon clicking, *The Kennedys* iPad app reveals a three-paneled user interface.

The first panel is a social feed on the screen's left side that lets users toggle between Facebook and Twitter. The tweet box comes prepopulated with #TheKennedys hashtag, making it effortless to contribute to the miniseries' backchannel conveniently displayed, in real-time, directly underneath. Embedding the backchannel into the iPad app itself eliminates the need to switch back and forth between Twitter (or Facebook) and the companion app—thereby providing a much more cohesive user experience.

The application's middle panel is a visual timeline of key events displayed as a set of thumbnails with dates and short descriptions. Clicking the oval-shaped "SYNC WITH REELZ TV" button at the top of the timeline displays the current runtime of the live broadcast, and re-sorts the timeline of events based on what is currently being aired on TV. As key events take place, they are stacked onto the timeline with their supporting media displaying in the rightmost panel.

For instance, in the first episode of the series, John F. Kennedy comes home to the family's compound in Hyannis Port, Massachusetts, after sustaining injuries by rescuing the crew of the sinking Navy vessel PT-109. As the events unfold within the television broadcast, the timeline feature of *The Kennedys* second screen app updates itself with "JFK Awarded Purple Heart" and displays a photo along with a short description. A series of "resource links" bring users to supplemental curated Web content including YouTube videos, photos, and other online information.

The two-screen experience of *The Kennedys* makes for a rich history lesson because of the way in which it was executed across second screen devices (including the laptop and smartphone) by connecting a very relevant content stream to the TV broadcast and its backchannel. Best of all, the companion experience is packaged in such a way where everything cleanly displays upfront.

A TV Event without a Second Screen Experience Is Like a Zebra without Stripes

Very few tentpole television events take place these days that do not include some sort of second screen experience. For example, NBC's coverage of the Royal Wedding included an iPad app fraught with content—including a visual tree of the royal family complete with detailed bios, as well as an interactive map of the wedding procession with context about each of its surrounding landmarks.[21] The iPad app had over 200,000 downloads with over 26,000 occurring the day of the wedding.[22]

Additionally, the *2011 Oscars* Backstage Pass iPad app let users switch back and forth among nine live streaming camera feeds to accompany the show's broadcast. The app exhibited a map of the stage and surrounding areas that indicated where each of the cameras was placed by showing a play button. Pressing "play" would then activate the live video stream for the chosen camera among options that included a Backstage cam, Press Room cam, and the Control Booth cam. A similar experience presented itself during the live Red Carpet as well as the Governors Ball party.

While we addressed MTV's innovative use of the backchannel for the 2009 Video Music Awards in Chapter 1, the 2011 VMA second screen experience was extended to the iPad and included a "Hot Seat" feature that, when selected, pulled up a seating chart of the Nokia Theatre where the VMAs took place. Each time a celebrity tweeted from their respective seat, the chart would indicate through a pulsating beacon from where in the theater and whom it was coming. Users could then interact with the visualized seating chart to drill down into specific celebrity tweets in real-time.

Do TV Viewers Value a Second Screen App More Than the Native Backchannel?

The most important thing about these products right now is that we can create a curated, important conversation with people of influence versus some sort of fire hose that provides a less meaningful conversation.

—Lisa Hsia, Executive Vice-President of Digital
Media at Bravo

Bravo was yet again the first TV network to launch a second screen iPad app. "Bravo Now" made its debut on Apple's App Store in August of 2010 to coincide with the season finale of *Bethenny Getting Married?*[23] At its core, the app serves as a companion to Bravo's linear television programming, enabling users to view, interact, and share additional content while watching certain Bravo TV show premieres and finales live.

Bravo enhanced its popular "talk bubble" for the iPad experience, with a timeline toward the top of the live events screen on the Bravo Now application. As the live show airs, a series of talk bubble icons appear, each of which denotes a particular media type relevant to the episode's content at a given moment. A talk bubble can be either a video clip, photo, poll, "fun fact," or a post from one of the "Bravolebrities."

Additionally, a real-time social stream appears along the entire left side that defaults to Twitter (and Facebook) posts from "Bravolebrities" who are live tweeting during the show, thereby granting users access to the insiders' live commentary. If they wish, viewers can toggle to the entire backchannel conversation from all who use the app to comment through an embedded Twitter and Facebook client.

Integrating the backchannel into second screen applications brings up an important question and point raised by *Lost Remote's* Cory Bergman:

Why wouldn't I use Facebook or Twitter proper to converse with my friends about a television show, instead of using a second screen experience that uses a Twitter client or a Facebook client that is not nearly as easy-to-use? In this case, you've got to make the second screen experience better by offering something else that's really exceptional—like a filtered community, insider knowledge, or a celebrity that's tweeting along with you. There has to be some unique hook.

The "hook" for Bravo Now includes access to synched companion content via its Talk Bubble, as well as a curated real-time social stream with filtering that allows for easy following of the commentary from the show's talent.

Each Network Approaches the Second Screen from a Slightly Different Angle

NBC's spin on its second screen companion app is the notion of a *host*, an NBC moderator who helps keep the conversation going by answering fan questions and adding live commentary. "NBC Live" was launched in May of 2011 and was enabled for four shows during the fall 2011 season. NBC's hope is that the app will help to drive original airtime viewing. In fact, 47 percent of respondents of an NBC Live Tracking Study indicated that they are more likely to watch NBC shows when they first air because of the NBC Live app.

The Discovery Channel launched an iPad app in March of 2011[24] and re-released it to include a second screen coviewing feature on July 31, 2011 to coincide with its ever-popular annual Shark Week.[25] In addition to exclusive interactive content, the Discovery Channel HD app includes a location-based TV schedule that automatically serves up show information based on one's physical geography.

Other second screen apps within our "network-specific" category include MTV's Watch With, HBO Connect, and USA's Character

Chatter that lives on the network's website as well as certain USA series' Facebook pages.[26] While television networks continue to build and enhance their own companion applications, other players in the market are developing solutions that work across networks. It is too early to tell which is better, and *Variety* magazine's Andrew Wallenstein raises the question that stakeholders in the space continue to ask:

> Is there going to be one central hub for these experiences to play out or is it going to be sort of like a Tower of Babel that provides thousands of apps that all essentially deliver companion experiences but on their own respective shows or networks? Everyone is struggling with this question right now, and there is no easy answer.

As is the case with all new media, the space tends to get very crowded and more complicated before clear leaders, standards, and interoperability truly emerge and take hold.

The Social TV Space Continues to Blend

Social TV app Miso—which we discussed in the last chapter in the context of TV check-ins—announced a second screen partnership with DirectTV in September of 2011.[27] DirectTV customers can now use the Miso application to interface with their DirectTV receiver to automatically display the show they are currently watching on the second screen. As the television viewer flips through or changes the channel, Miso automatically updates itself to deliver a synchronized companion TV experience.

Their first major deployment using synched content happened on October 2, 2011, during the season six premiere of Showtime's *Dexter*.[28] iPhone Miso users who watched the show via DirectTV benefited from a synched stream of enhanced content, including Wikipedia articles about actors and guest stars when they first appeared, as well as quotes, trivia, and other lean-forward content that utilized Miso's Pick 'em functionality. Miso times a piece of content to be pushed out against the exact moment within the show's storyline in order to increase the content's relevance. By leveraging native iOS push notifications, Miso is able to alert its users each time they deliver a new piece of content during the show versus adding to the distraction away from the main television screen.

In May of 2011, Miso released a report detailing the company's findings from a second screen experiment it conducted with Boxee (a connected TV device we discuss in Chapter 9). "Miso Sync," as it was called, delivered *Pop-Up Video* style experiences to TV viewers watching content through the Boxee Box. The experiment sought to answer three questions: Do people want information while they watch TV? What type of information do they want? Is the second screen a passive or active vehicle?[29]

The experiment ran for four weeks and used a cross-section of six second screen-enabled TV shows varying in genre and length. One of Miso's most substantial findings—based on its user sample's behaviors and feedback—is that every type of show requires a unique second-screen experience in terms of the companion content's type, frequency, delivery, and timing. For instance, Miso found that the kind of information to which users responded most powerfully for reality shows was gossip and candid images delivered at a high frequency, mostly during the show itself. When it came to dramas, on the other hand, users wanted to see high-quality images and memorable moments at a much lower frequency before and after the show, but not as much during (with the exception of commercials).

Miso's perspective is that all TV shows can have a second screen experience as long as that experience fits with the show's tone, pace, and style. And as more and more companion platforms are created and gain momentum, they become increasingly valuable to advertisers.

On the Second Screen, Content and Advertising Can Work Really Well Together

The Holy Grail for all this has been, for so many years, to have a feedback loop with television. So that when I'm watching something, I am able to not only interact with the TV show; I can also interact with the ads. That's always been what interactive TV has promised, but has never delivered on. When that happens on a truly scaled basis, there will be so much new value creation in this business that it will really be the second coming of television.

—Cory Bergman, Founder of *Lost Remote*

TV networks are experimenting with different advertising models built into their companion applications. For instance, the ABC *Grey's Anatomy* application is sold as a single sponsorship with 100 percent share-of-voice and allows for a trivia question module or information (video) module that appears, in-line, during commercial breaks of the show. In contrast, the NBC Live app serves up clickable banner ads and also runs interstitial video ads that are timed to appear as the TV show that is being watched cuts to a commercial break. The NBC Live virtual host will also post right before or right after an ad runs about the given sponsor.

Each of the network apps offers slightly different opportunities that continue to evolve based on application enhancements and ad performance findings—which is why advertisers must always adopt a "test and learn" attitude when approaching the second screen. As *Variety's* Andrew Wallenstein explains:

I don't think the second screen companion experience is truly anywhere near critical mass. But it's very much in the interest of the networks to encourage usage; not just because it deepens the experience but because the true brass ring is the ability to serve ads on more than one platform. It changes the nature of the ads because they will be interactive on the second screen. While I think that is something that could be a huge game changer, I don't think it's "in the bag" by any means. Advertisers have the potential to be the straw that stirs this drink. If they can drive the innovation, there's no question that the programmers will get on board. But from my vantage point, I see the programmers trying to get the advertisers on board.

Brands who evaluate the scale and reach of a companion app solely by itself fail to consider how people experience media. The second screen is a great opportunity for advertisers who look at their television media buy as an integrated cross-channel experience where each component (or screen) works together—thus making the advertising much more impactful.

A great example of this is Verizon's sponsorship of *The X Factor*. The show's creator and lead judge, Simon Cowell, is featured in Verizon Wireless TV spots, during the show's commercial breaks, that promote the "Xtra Factor" second screen app which is also "presented by" Verizon.

The iPad version syncs with *The X Factor's* on-air broadcast with interactive content, trivia, and the ability to rate each contestant's performance. The Android version of the Verizon-influenced app enables users to cast a legitimate vote for their favorite contestant with merely a single click. [30]

Verizon approached its media buy with Fox not as a traditional television *watching* advertising strategy, but instead as a television *experiencing* strategy. The result is an "everywhere brand" in that Verizon transcends all of the media channels wherein viewers experience *The X Factor*.

The Next Evolution of Second Screen Advertising Is Synched Ads

We are pioneering a new advertising medium called the sync ad. In essence, you have a TV spot on the first screen doing what it does well—which is to provide a sense of emotion and immediacy—and

then at the same moment, you have on the second screen a digital
ad that does what digital ads do well—provide interaction, trans-
actions, and data collection.

—Seth Tapper, Founder and CEO at
SecondScreen Networks

Advertising group SecondScreen Networks is looking to be the modern day DoubleClick for the social and companion TV space. They are seeking to power second screen experiences in a truly synched way as viewers engage with television.

The company's technology essentially watches TV through its server-side automated content recognition platform.[31] When an advertiser's commercial begins airing, the platform sends a notification to all second screens that comprise the ad buy to run the appropriate synched digital ad, which appears within a quarter of a second of the broadcast spot's start time.

For example, on September 14, 2011, USA Network partnered with SecondScreen Networks to run a Lincoln-Mercury branded synch ad during the season one finale of *Necessary Roughness*. USA Network created the rich media "polling" ad, which was served on its Character Chatter companion app at the exact moment Lincoln-Mercury's TV spot aired. SecondScreen Networks reported early results that showed the Sync Ad garnering engagement rates at "an order of magnitude" higher than traditional (nonsync) ad units.

In all likelihood, the two-screen synched ad experience has a higher audience receptivity rate, given the companion reinforcement of the broadcast message. The key factor in making this work, however, is establishing a very large base of second screen partnerships within the ad network in order to increase the chances of the synched scenario playing out. It is a bit of a chicken-and-egg scenario, as Seth points out:

There is no second screen experience that really has a substantial audience. The advertisers who are relevant in the sync ad space are advertisers who buy television commercials—which means they are looking for mass reach. On the other side of the coin, none of the second screen experiences have anything like mass reach yet.

In the meantime, SecondScreen Networks is laying the infrastructure for synched ads across devices and websites, as companion application audiences continue to grow and the space matures.

Buy or Build? Some Brands Have Built Their Own Second Screen Experiences

On April 26, 2011, Heineken launched its "StarPlayer" iPhone app, which acts as a branded second screen companion while watching UEFA Champions League matches on TV.[32] The concept was inspired by the fact that over a billion people worldwide watch soccer. The application, which can also be played online, is based on the premise of predicting scores and other events during a given soccer match. For instance, a user who thinks their team is going to score within the next 30 seconds can click a "goal now" button. If the team scores in time, the user earns points and can compare their real-time scores with others who are playing along.

Built-in Facebook integrations within the Heineken app enable users to share their activity; the beer company also serves up bonus trivia questions during slower periods of the match. The app is a powerful way to sustain a constant stream of branded engagement over the course of a 90-minute match. In June of 2011, AKQA—the agency behind the application—won a Gold Lion at the 58th Cannes Lions International Festival of Creativity in France, one of the most renowned advertising competitions.[33] It is simply yet another example of the rapid innovation that continues to take place within the second screen space.

TAKE ACTION: THE SECOND SCREEN

When audiences engage with television in a lean-forward manner, they use the second screen in a way that puts them in a much more active state of mind. The following are three ways to reach your target by leveraging the second screen with your television media buy.

1. *Embrace the distraction.* It is important to acknowledge that not everyone is watching your TV spots during commercial breaks. If you are able to recognize the distraction, you suddenly open the doors to an unlimited amount of resonant cross-channel content possibilities. You need not sacrifice your goals on the main TV screen when incorporating the second screen into your creative concepts.

2. *Let the two screens have a "play date."* The power of the second screen is that it acts as a companion to the main television broadcast, thereby making the whole experience greater than the sum of its two parts. This should be no different for your broadcast advertising. Work with the television networks or second screen ad providers to let your TV and second screen ads "play nice" together to create a unified and synched cross-channel branded experience.

3. *Ask; don't tell.* The primary television screen is a one-way messaging system (although even that is beginning to change). The second screen, however, is two-way and interactive. Simple banner ads and video preroll are just more methods of one-way telling. Your brand's second screen content should be designed for the medium on which it is displayed. So *ask* people to engage with your brand by giving them an inviting reason to do so.

Distraction Is Not Going Away

In fact, distraction to advertising will only intensify as technology (especially mobile and tablet devices) continues to evolve. The irony in all of this is that some of the companion experiences with which television networks are experimenting to help increase tune-in are actually fueling the distraction *away* from their commercial breaks. The key is to capture and harness this distraction to ensure your brand is making a resonant impact on all screens.

Scan for More

Scan this QR code using your mobile device for videos and visuals of the examples and cases referenced throughout this chapter.

Don't have a smartphone with a QR reader app? No problem. You can access companion content directly by going to http://www .socialtvbook.net/tagged/chapter4.

5

Social TV Ratings

Adding a New Dimension to Television Audience Measurement

Computer geek turned secret agent Chuck Bartowski made his character debut on September 24, 2007. NBC's one-hour action comedy *Chuck* quickly found itself an extremely loyal following.

In its series premiere, a sequence of events is set into motion when Chuck's former college roommate-turned-CIA agent Bryce sends him an encoded e-mail. After cracking the puzzle, Chuck suddenly finds himself with the US Government's top NSA and CIA intelligence downloaded to his brain. This set the stage for a television series plot that would give its audience an interesting combination of action, adventure, mystery, and comedy. *Chuck* premiered with over nine million viewers[1] watching—a number that represented the highest ratings the series has garnered to date.

Toward the end of *Chuck's* second season, NBC announced a radical strategic shift to its primetime programming format for the upcoming 2009 fall television season. Late night program host Jay Leno would be leaving *The Tonight Show* in favor of a one-hour primetime series simply called *The Jay Leno Show*.[2] In order to accommodate this change, NBC would be canceling five of its scripted series—and *Chuck* was, as the television industry says, "on the bubble."

Chuck's audience size had steadily dropped by an estimated average of 1,200,000 viewers between the first and second season.[3] There were reports that NBC.com was referencing *Chuck's* season two finale as a series finale.[4] *Chuck's* feverishly passionate fans refused to merely sit idly by and wait for NBC's decision. Instead, they would end up proving themselves as a force to be reckoned with.

Viewers took to the Web and launched a full-fledged campaign in hopes of convincing NBC to renew *Chuck* for a third season. While there were many online petitions, discussion groups, forums, blog posts, and videos that made their appeal, one site in particular helped to lead the charge. On April 6, 2009, GiveMeMyRemote.com released a post whose title gave a nod to the "Nerd Herd"—the name of Chuck's technical support team at fictitious electronics store "Buy More."[5]

"Be a Nerd . . . Join the Herd. Save CHUCK." The simple yet powerful mantra provided *Chuck* viewers with an arsenal of resources to help get new people to watch the show and increase its Nielsen ratings—the very measure that television networks use to determine a TV show's success. If fans could spread the word to tune in and "save Chuck" for the second season's remaining three episodes, perhaps that could help augment the show's viewership. Among the hundreds of comments left on the post was the following from "StephanieP," who wrote:

> I cannot imagine what a world without Chuck would be like! It always helps me to get through Mondays. Using word of mouth IS an effective way to get people to watch Chuck. I started watching last year after a friend of mine told me about [it]. Then this season I got another friend interested. Now all three of us get together every week and watch.

The "Save Chuck" campaign encouraged show fans to use their Facebook status updates to express their love for *Chuck* and to remind friends to tune in to the show at eight o'clock every Monday. Downloadable "Save Chuck" postcards, badges, and Twitter backgrounds were created, and fans encouraged one another to retweet any *Chuck*-related blog posts. A #SaveChuck hashtag was quickly adopted as a real-time conversation connector on Twitter, enabling anyone to easily follow along and participate on the popular microblogging platform.[6]

In addition to vying for NBC's attention, fans also gave their support to advertiser Subway (whose brand is frequently integrated into the show) by rallying the public to go to their nearest Subway, buy a footlong sub, and thank the company for supporting *Chuck*.[7] Helping the cause was *Chuck* star Zachary Levi who led a group of hundreds of convention-goers in the United Kingdom to their local Subway on April 26, 2009. "Inundate the Internet. Let it get all over the place. It seems pretty apropos to me to get a whole convention of nerds, like myself, to sell out a Subway," Zach said in front of the crowd.[8] Once there, Zack even got behind the popular submarine sandwich shop's counter himself to help manage the friendly mob.

The day of reckoning came on May 19, 2009 when NBC released a statement announcing that it had made the decision to renew *Chuck* for a third season. "Renewal Represents Triumph for Fans and TV Critics Who Waged Successful Online and Twitter 'Save Chuck' Campaign Supported by Subway" read the subheading on the NBC press release.[9] Not only did the network acknowledge the groundswell of fan support; it also managed to strike an upfront advertising deal with Subway to help finance *Chuck*'s third season.

Nielsen Is the Currency by Which Advertisers and TV Networks Transact

The default mechanism is absolutely the Nielsen rating. We wake up to that report card every single morning and it is still a very useful tool.
> —Geri Wang, President of Sales and Marketing at ABC

In 1950, Nielsen, the global information and measurement company, took the audience measurement methodologies that it had developed for radio and adapted them for the emerging and growing medium of television.[10] While many people today might think of Nielsen as a ratings company, it is, in effect, the arbiter of most of the advertising that goes through our video screens across platforms, and a significant provider of marketing and consumer information. As Nielsen's Senior Vice President of Media and Agency Insights Jon Gibs illustrated for us:

> Our TV ratings are the industry standard for buying and selling television advertising; they essentially dictate how dollars and cents are traded within the TV industry. For much of

Nielsen's history, the TV-side of the business was almost more of an auditing company whose job was to present numbers in-market that advertisers and TV networks could use to transact.

As such, Nielsen has to undergo a rigorous auditing process and be held accountable to the numbers on which they report, since "billions upon billions" of dollars are at stake. Given that businesses rely on these figures as a means by which to make major media buys, the data behind them must be nothing short of absolutely dependable.

To get an idea of how the process works—a single Nielsen ratings point equates to 1 percent of all US households with television sets.[11] So, a rating of 6.0 for a given TV show means that an estimated 6 percent of all TV households tuned into that show. Nielsen recalculates this number—which is currently at 114,600,000[12]—each August to prepare for the new fall TV season.

While the source for Nielsen's television ratings system started out as self-reported data from handwritten diaries, the 1990s introduced "set meters" physically connected to television sets. They are now able to report minute-by-minute ratings based on viewers' channel surfing behaviors within the company's sample set for Nielsen's national markets.

Since then, Nielsen has also created its "C3 rating," representing the audience size for a given TV show's commercial time. This is defined by the average of all of the commercial minutes within a TV episode, plus three days of commercial viewing during time-shifted (DVR) playback. Any fast forwarding of commercials within the three-day window is excluded from the ratings calculation.

While Nielsen data is not perfect, changing the way in which the ratings system gets modeled and measured is a far more complicated endeavor than it appears on the surface. Though the Holy Grail data source is, of course, households' set-top boxes, this approach comes with numerous constraints. One in particular is outdated hardware and lack of connectivity, which prevents speedy progress down this path. Hundreds of siloed systems would need to be stitched together before this could even start to happen. In addition, set-top box data alone is not necessarily a complete answer. It currently cannot report on the demographics of who within the household is watching and whether or not the television set was actually turned on since today's cable boxes tend not to be powered off.

Given the importance and need for both consistency and reliability of Nielsen data, the company will always err on the side of extreme caution as it considers how the process of rating television is evolving. And while TV networks continue to value Nielsen as the de facto standard when measuring their programming's performance, the emergence of social media has given them another dimension to consider. We call this the "social rating."

Social Media Creates a Feedback Loop for Television

We as a network believe the value of our brand is beyond just the C3 rating. We are now able to assemble a presentation about a show, like Gossip Girl, *and paint a much broader picture so that we're able to qualify, in some way, that the show is much bigger than just the Nielsen measurement.*

— Alison Tarrant, EVP Integrated Sales
and Marketing at The CW

We discussed in the first chapter how the backchannel is bringing people back to watching television live again. Chapter 3 examined the TV check-in landscape and we demonstrated in the previous chapter how the second screen has become a companion to television. All of these social TV activities are taking place *while* people are watching television—and, in the process, are creating lots of raw data as viewers engage.

Tweets per second, volume of show mentions, number of check-ins, amount of posts, and conversation sentiment are just a few of the metrics that social media produces to which television networks have easy access. This, in turn, gives networks information in addition to (although not in *replacement* of) Nielsen ratings. Social media can help to add in color where Nielsen cannot in order to reveal nonapparent insights. This was the case for ABC's *Castle* as Rick Mandler, ABC's Vice President of Digital Media, explained to us:

> Though *Castle* was a success coming out of the gate, it was not a huge success—yet it was very strong online. That showed us that there was an audience for the show and that we needed to get behind it and be patient—and that proved to work out for the best.

Since a growing amount of television networks are turning to social media for insights, we wondered whether or not this would begin to affect how the industry thinks about television ratings. However, Nielsen executive Jon Gibs was very clear about the fact that a TV rating is very distinct from a social rating—and that the two are unlikely to blend to become one:

> There's no specific reason to account for social media within TV ratings which are a specific thing: namely, the number of people who watch a program. Nowadays, there's a need in the market to understand the impact of social on driving the amount of people that watch TV, so that a TV broadcaster as a marketer can understand how to engage with social media in order to get more people to watch their program. But there's no real need to actually enhance a TV rating itself—specifically with social media data.

While the Nielsen rating will not change to incorporate the notion of a social rating, there is no denying that insights from social media continue to grow in value as a source of information to both television networks and TV advertisers. The question that continues to be on everyone's minds, however, has to do with the relationship between the two.

Does Social Media Engagement Correlate to Ratings?

Back in October of 2010, we did a small experiment to see if there was a relationship between the degree of backchannel conversation during new fall TV premieres versus their resulting Nielsen ratings and, hence, audience size.[13] Since over one-third of new television shows get canceled each year, we wondered if we could use this data to predict which ones may be at risk.

We looked at data from 19 different TV show premieres using popular social media monitoring tool Radian6 to extract backchannel tweets that took place during each of the respective shows' premiere episodes. Using easily accessible Twitter data made the most sense, given the fact that tweets are public and therefore provided us with a consistent and standardized backchannel source.

For each show premiere, we compared volume of Twitter mentions with the episode's number of Nielsen broadcast impressions. We also used Radian6 to sample positive sentiment before, during, and after each premiere, and tracked any change in this using a line graph. While we recognize that autosentiment analysis is far from perfect, it gave us a directional baseline by which to compare across shows.

As we looked at the data, we noticed that CBS's *Hawaii Five-0* premiere was one that immediately stood out as having both the highest impressions as well as Twitter volume across our sample of shows. It also was one of the few new fall TV shows where positive sentiment continued to increase as the show progressed and thereafter.

On the other side of the spectrum fell NBC's *Outlaw*, which had both low broadcast impressions and low Twitter mentions. Its level of positive sentiment was relatively high before the show began, had an ever-so-slight increase at the episode start, and then dwindled down midway and beyond. It was not surprising to us when NBC announced *Outlaw*'s cancellation shortly thereafter.

While the extreme cases (in which the two data points together were either high or low) were fairly clear cut in determining whether or not the show would survive, most shows were not as black and white. NBC's *Undercovers* was the only show premiere in our sample where Twitter mentions visually outnumbered broadcast impressions on our chart (broadcast impressions were expressed in millions). The show's overall positive sentiment was moderately good as it settled back down to preshow levels after getting a notable bump during the broadcast. Despite the high volume of Twitter mentions with modest ratings, NBC announced *Undercovers'* cancellation after only seven episode airings.

Law and Order LA, on the other hand, was the exact mirror opposite. Its premiere episode garnered extremely high broadcast impressions with only a medium amount of Twitter mentions that produced decreasing positive sentiment as the show aired. Regardless, its minimal social media chatter simply did not matter, since *Law and Order* is what we like to call a "Nielsen ratings machine." It is also one that reiterates this book's consistent theme that scripted dramas tend to produce lower volume backchannels during show airings.

So in the end, the burning question on everyone's mind is: Does the social media conversation drive TV ratings? The answer is that there is no scientific proof that makes a direct and exact conclusion—*yet*.

Television Networks Are Seeing a Relationship

We're hearing more frequently that producers have changed the live television event layout to actually drive more tweeting early on to help compel the highest possible rating. You used to hold your biggest acts until later in the show. But instead, Lady Gaga opened the 2011 VMAs, whereas she would normally have done her act at the half way or the two thirds mark in the past. Producers now want to get the Twitter ripple going early and then play it out.

—Chloe Sladden, Director of Content and Programming at Twitter

While science has yet to indisputably prove a direct correlation between the size of a TV series' backchannel and its resulting ratings, more and more people within the television industry are pointing to anecdotal evidence. Even Radha Subramanyam, Nielsen's SVP of Consumer Insights and Analytics, admits to us that there has to be *some* kind of relationship; it is just not one that can be simply defined "across the board":

> A few years ago, people were claiming that 'social media and TV have no relationship at all. One has nothing to do with the other; so let's just ignore it and see what happens.' Then there was the other extreme school of thought that came up in the past year or two where people believe that 'every rating point and everything that happens in television comes as result of a friend referral or something that happened in social media.' And that's obviously not true either. We're seeing that there are obviously relationships, because these are two of the biggest areas in which people spend time in life and in culture; but they aren't simple relationships. Relationships vary quite significantly by age, in some cases by gender—and they vary a lot by the type of content.

One such content type is clearly reality competitions, such as *The Voice*, which we profiled in Chapter 1. The program enjoyed remarkable integrated social media success, and the volume of backchannel conversation was incredibly high. NBC tracked the Nielsen rating as the show progressed while monitoring its social conversation, and network Senior Vice President of Strategic Digital and Broadcast Marketing Research Julie DeTraglia shared with us that there was a distinct relationship between Twitter mentions and *The Voice*'s ratings increases during the show's premiere episode:

> It's very difficult to quantify the fact that any change you see in TV ratings comes from social media activity. But *The Voice* is a great example of an instance in which we did a tremendous

amount of social outreach beforehand and then utilized a persistent Twitter hashtag that really helped to drive the conversation. We saw all of this Twitter activity during the premiere, and the ratings went up over the course of the night through each quarter hour. While we can't directly connect it, it's hard to deny there was some power at work.

And the evidence continues to build. On October 6, 2011, Nielsen released results of a study it conducted across 250 television shows in which they analyzed how lifts in online show-related buzz connects with ratings. Nielsen concluded that not only *was* there a relationship, but they were even able to quantify it most significantly around premiere episodes. They found that a 9 percent increase in buzz a few weeks prior to a show's premiere equates to a 1 percent ratings point increase. For midseason episodes and finales, an online conversation lift of 14 percent is needed to accomplish a similar ratings increase.[14]

Since our own experiment back in 2010, companies who specialize in social TV ratings—and who use far more advanced methods of data collection and distillation—have emerged. While key television industry stakeholders can now utilize these tools to more readily gain access to data at a much greater scale, we are just at the beginning of the story that defines what social ratings actually mean—and how best to make them actionable.

Bluefin Analyzes the Relationships between Impressions and Expressions

Imagine a machine that watches all television, listens to the world's public social conversations, and connects the dots to create an insight engine that can be used to drive real-time decision-making where the integrity of the data is measurably sufficient that you can trust billions of dollars to be touched by that data.

—Deb Roy, Cofounder and CEO at Bluefin Labs

Bluefin came out of "stealth mode" in February of 2011 and introduced one of its first products, called Bluefin Signals, which produces social TV analytics relevant to television networks, brands, and advertising agencies. Its system software, born out of MIT's media lab, has a number of inputs, including a satellite television feed that is literally watching television around the clock and digitally fingerprinting the content as it processes it. The closed captioning feed is another input that feeds the vocal dialog within a TV show verbatim, which can then be cross-referenced with the real-time social backchannel in order to make direct attributions to the given show.

When you add the channel guide data provided by Tribune Media to all of this, you have an incredibly tight system offered by Bluefin—one that analyzes communication patterns and data-driven context to define (with a fair amount of certainty) the probability that a tweet or public Facebook post relates to a specific television broadcast's content.

With fingerprinting on over 200 US broadcast and cable networks that represents over 210,000 individual telecasts, Bluefin is able to semantically analyze beyond TV *impressions* to understand the *expressions* consumers generate as they remark on content they are watching. As Bluefin's cofounder and CEO Deb Roy explained to us:

You have a piece of television content that radiates through television networks and it makes impressions on members of an audience. People have always talked about what they watch on TV. As long as there've been TV impressions, TV has always translated into social expressions; so the general pattern is impressions in, expressions out. But a lot of those expressions now have their own networks through which to radiate. Therefore, just like the TV content radiates through television networks to people, those people's social expressions are now radiating through the social graph to other people. So expressions are making impressions. If you and I were sitting on a couch together watching TV and I turn to you and mutter something, then my expression made an impression—end of story. But instead, I tweet it, and who knows how far and how long that expression will go. It's that seepage of private into public—and once it becomes public, you add to that another layer of technology such as Bluefin—this ability, at scale, to start understanding the cause and effect relationships between impressions and expressions. And that is what we think is the game changer.

When one logs into Bluefin Signals, they first see a Summary Dashboard that displays a comparative view of television network trends (displayed as a line graph) over the past 30 days. Appearing below the trends are the most popular shows listed and grouped by broadcast and cable channels. Though the list defaults to the past week, it can also be toggled to filter by alternative date options. At the time that this was written, the top shows appearing within the Summary Dashboard include *Monday Night Football* on ESPN, *Glee* on Fox, and *The X Factor* on Fox (whose "social rating" score was tied with *Jersey Shore* on MTV).

The entire dashboard is fraught with rollovers and drilldowns that provide expansive data mining capabilities that expose a deeper level of information and insight. For example, users can view verbatim expressions for each show along with a tag cloud of popular keywords. Past conversation levels as well as connections to other TV shows are also available. Table views are easily sorted, and data can be exported to Excel for further manipulation.

Beyond the Summary Dashboard, an Audience Response feature lets users analyze metrics that include share of conversation and gender grouped by TV networks, individual shows, or genres within a specified date range. A number of filters are available for each of the data views, including dayparts and genres.

Bluefin Signals' Audience Connection feature visually maps out show-to-show or brand-to-show relationships using its data. For instance, of the set of people that Bluefin has identified as discussing hit show *Glee* during and around the time that an episode aired (using an arbitrary week that we chose), there was also a strong affinity by many of those same people for programs *Raising Hope* and *Karaoke Battle USA* during that same week. Bluefin is able to interpret and make these kinds of connections within the back-channel conversation.

A similar methodology also works for brands. A Bluefin Signals user can type in the name of a brand and see the top television shows discussed among those who also discussed the brand during the given time period. Using the same week from our *Glee* example, we can also see that a popular QSR brand that will remain nameless has a strong affinity connection to *Boardwalk Empire* and the television broadcasts of movies *The Terminal* and *Batman Begins*.

In addition to brand names, Bluefin Signals can be mined by certain audience types such as "parents" or "coffee drinkers." This level of data-driven insight, at scale, is immensely powerful in the hands of TV networks who are seeking to uncover new advertisers, as well as brands trying to determine where else to buy ad space. It is highly unlikely that traditional methods used to do either task would yield the same results set. This should not be seen as alarming; instead it should be considered an opportunity to look at media and marketing plans differently by expanding the inputs used to inform them. The data that is generated by the collective mass of "social impressions" can now be used as a means to augment existing methods of insight gathering and decision making.

Trendrr Was the First to Market with Social TV Ratings Charts

Real-time data informs the TV stack in multiple ways. It informs it from the research perspective, and from an adverting and ad sales perspective. It informs it from a ratings and engagement perspective as well as from a production perspective. Each way is unique.

—Mark Ghuneim, CEO and Cofounder at Trendrr

Back in 2005, Trendrr was known as Infofilter, a company focused predominantly on providing social media listening insights for marketers and agencies based on analytics from social bookmarking and photo sharing sites Delicious and Flickr (since Twitter did not exist at the time). Over the past several years, Trendrr grew its social media monitoring solution, and on April 4, 2011, they launched Trendrr.tv, making them the first to market with a specific product for "social TV ratings" in a chart form.

Trendrr.tv is currently powered using "fire hose" data from Twitter as well as check-in data from Miso and GetGlue, combined with public Facebook status updates. The site's free Social Television Charts display the top 10 cable and broadcast shows as measured by total activity of tweets, Facebook posts, and TV check-ins. Users can toggle back and forth between Trendrr.tv's daily or weekly charts depending on their preferred snapshot of data.

In addition to providing a given show's "social rating," Trendrr reports on the positive versus negative sentiment and activity loss or gain from the previous reporting period. While there are options to drill down into more detailed information, individuals must have a paid subscription to the service to actually do so. The subscription allows users to access detailed show pages that break out activity by social network as well as gender. Two visual graphs display the program's Twitter activity through two viewing options of 24 hours or 30 days. Top geographic markets are also listed in rank order by the amount of activity that a given show produces. Top Twitter influencers—measured by their respective Klout scores (which is a measure of influence based on one's social engagement and amplification) are also included.

Trendrr allows its users to slice and mine its data on a macro level in a variety of ways, using a range of filters and sort functions. Additionally, by using natural language processing, Trendrr.tv is able to forecast most anticipated shows and help to elicit buzz about major tentpole TV events. For instance, toward the beginning of September of 2011, Trendrr.tv began publishing its list of most discussed fall TV pilots leading up to their premieres.[15] Early frontrunners included (in order): *Once Upon a Time* on ABC, *The Playboy Club* on NBC, *Revenge* on ABC, *Charlie's Angels* on ABC, and *The Secret Circle* on The CW.

Trendrr.tv also provides a set of curation tools that it uses in partnerships like "The Weather Channel Social," announced in August of 2011.[16] Based in part on the insight that Twitter users in the United States send about 200 weather-related tweets per minute (which can more-than-double on active weather days), the partnership brings tweets on-air as well as within The Weather Channel's online and mobile properties. Trendrr uses its social intelligence system to classify tweets to ensure they are actually about the weather, determine location, and filter out profanity.[17]

While Trendrr and Bluefin both offer solutions that produce social TV ratings, the resulting output can vary between the two due to their differences in data sources and algorithms. For instance, Trendrr reports *Glee* as the top broadcast and *Jersey Shore* as the top cable show, while Bluefin reports NFL Football and the GOP Debate, respectively—when comparing the same, randomly selected, week.

SocialGuide Is More Than a Social TV Guide, It Also Provides Social TV Ratings

I was looking at my Facebook and Twitter feeds and noticed that a lot of people were talking about TV, and that a lot of the conversation was about TV as TV was airing. I thought that if my friends and I are doing that for the shows we watch, it'd be interesting to find out how much conversation was happening across the entire linear TV landscape.

—Sean Casey, Founder and CEO at SocialGuide

Though we first introduced SocialGuide in Chapter 2 within the context of social TV guides, the company has a dual role operating as a solution for social TV ratings *and* social TV analytics. Similar to

Trendrr.tv's charts, SocialGuide publishes the Social 100, which is a publicly available ranking of the "100 most social programs" on television. It also publishes the most social in primetime, episodes, sports events, and networks. Using public application programming interfaces (APIs) from Facebook data and Twitter, SocialGuide's scope measures the social activity of 177 TV channels and on average measures over 4,000 unique programs per month—all of which is made possible by the company's partnership with Tribune Media (who also provides data to Bluefin Labs). The Social 100 is published weekly and monthly, while a top 10 list is posted daily on SocialGuide's website.[18]

The company also uses its data to power its enterprise-level social analytics tool called SocialGuide Intelligence, which allows users to view and mine of all the social activity that SocialGuide captures around US television programming. A user audience of TV networks, brands, and agencies is similarly defined by both Bluefin and Trendrr. SocialGuide Intelligence provides specific insight into social audience and influencers as well as offers network, program, and episode-level data.

What Is the Ultimate Value of High Social TV Ratings?

Measuring the conversation within social TV is a bit like the chicken and the egg situation: If you create something good on TV then, of course, people are going to talk about it. And if people start talking about it, of course, that stuff on TV is going to become amplified. So it's a bit of "which came first?" Most often, I think it's born out of good content on the TV screen itself.
—Ryan Osborn, Director of Social Media at NBC News

In Chapter 1, we discussed the value of social impressions given the fact that they come with an inherent endorsement. Although not all social impressions carry an equal amount of influence (something that also varies by who receives them), there is no doubt that the backchannel is an influential entity. And while TV networks want to know if fostering voluminous backchannel conversations about their shows is helping ratings, Bluefin Labs' Deb Roy shares another question for stakeholders to consider:

> Does more tweeting lead to higher ratings, meaning audience size? I understand why that's a significant point of interest. Another related question is: what does it mean when you get varying levels of remarkability for the same audience size? It's got to mean *something*. Let's say all being held equal: you know the demographics, you know everything you want to know about the people who are talking—and then you have two shows, each of which has 10 million viewers. In one case, 50,000 people talk; in another case, 500,000 talk. So what does that mean? And to whom? There are people on the content side, and then there are advertisers. I think it's got to mean something to each of them. If you like the answer that 500,000 means I get 10 times more something—which is of value to me—I'll then want to drive that number up, independent of impressions. It's not that I don't want more impressions as well; but they're separate dimensions in this scenario.

The more people that engage on TV's backchannel, the higher the chances others online will discover and tune in, out of curiosity, to the programming getting the lion's share of buzz. The other major value proposition is that large backchannels produce a goldmine of insights that are ready and waiting to be surfaced. If TV networks and advertisers are not quite ready to make the leap by claiming that social media is good for ratings, then they can at least benefit from social ratings data as an input to strategy and planning decisions.

Measuring the Backchannel Turns Raw Data into Useful Information

Bluefin took a look at the highest "social TV rated" episodes of a number of television shows (within the first three quarters of 2011) and examined what dominated the backchannel during the times that those particular episodes aired. The 6:00 PM (Eastern) airing of ESPN's *SportsCenter* on Sept 5, 2011 sparked its biggest backchannel conversation around the topic of Maryland's "ugly uniforms." The topic of same sex marriage in New York produced CNN's *Anderson Cooper 360*'s largest backchannel on June 24, 2011. And on May 2, 2011, TBS's *Conan* drove its highest social TV rating when guest star Will Ferrell shaved Conan's beard on-air.

Trendrr has found Hispanic/Latino American viewers to be a very vocal backchannel demographic. When comparing the social conversation levels between the Miss Universe versus Miss Universo pageants, Trendrr reported that the #missuniverso hashtag had three times the Twitter backchannel volume of the #missuniverse hashtag. Trendrr also compared the social ratings of *Glee*'s season two versus season three premieres to find a 40 percent drop in the size of the latter's Twitter backchannel, which also had a 29 percent drop in its Nielsen ratings.[19]

SocialGuide examined the season nine premiere of *Project Runway*, which aired on July 28, 2011, and found that 8 percent of the entire television backchannel conversation was about *Project Runway* during the time that it aired. Eighty percent of the *Project Runway* premiere episode mentions occurred within a four-hour window of its linear broadcast airing—with 53 percent of the total conversation taking place during the show itself. Twitter @replies made up the bulk of the conversation—a statistic that indicates that *Project Runway*'s backchannel was more of a back-and-forth virtual coviewing experience, versus a bunch of one-way self-expressions.

Of course, while all of this information is interesting—and would surely make for terrific PowerPoint eye candy—it provides little value if it is not actionable enough to help inform decisions.

How Advertisers Can Use the Backchannel's Insights for Decision Making

One of the ways that advertisers benefit most from social ratings tools is by measuring brand conversation lift and to find (and then target) engaged audiences. As we mentioned in Chapter 1, backchannel conversation is not limited to the television shows themselves; it also includes TV commercials.

For example—Diet Pepsi's "Beach Tweet" spot aired 746 times across 260 different television shows. Because Bluefin's video fingerprinting technology also encompasses commercials, they were able to isolate a control and exposed group in order to measure brand conversation lift.

The exposed group consisted of 1,800,000 people who watched and posted about any of the television shows wherein the Diet Pepsi commercial aired on the backchannel. The control group, which was comprised of 2,200,000 people, was defined similarly; however, it was done before the Diet Pepsi campaign began. By measuring pre- and post-brand mentions for "Diet Pepsi" within the backchannel, Bluefin was able to calculate a 19 percent brand conversation lift among the exposed audience. This kind of measurement begins to leverage the notion of a feedback loop the likes of which television has traditionally never had.

This leads into the second key social ratings use case for advertisers. We are all aware by now that certain kinds of TV shows are more apt to generate fuller bodied backchannels. As Nielsen's Radha Subramanyam puts it, "Social has varying impact depending on the kind of content you have. If it's a broadcast drama, it may be a very successful show; but chances are the extra lift you get from social is going to be less."

The same is true for television commercials. Brands that integrate lean-forward experiences into their TV spot creative are much more apt to have greater participatory success when placed in target-appropriate, lean-forward television shows. Once a TV viewer is already engaged on the second screen due to the nature of the actual program, they do not have to mentally (or physically) shift gears when an equally matched lean-forward TV commercial follows.

Using social TV ratings tools to find and assess lean-forward versus lean-back television programming gives media planners and buyers another dimension on which to evaluate advertising opportunities based on a campaign's objectives and the nature of its creative.

We can take this idea a step further by mapping and analyzing affinity relationships. In the case of the Diet Pepsi Beach Tweet example, Bluefin found two times the amount of brand mentions on television shows where its Signals product revealed a high affinity for Diet Pepsi versus low affinity shows where the TV spot also aired.

While social TV ratings charts give people a sense of the television shows that produce the biggest backchannels, it is important to keep in mind that those shows may not be appropriate for a particular brand's target, message, or core values. By using tools that map affinity relationships, advertisers are able to get brand-specific social TV ratings that are far more valuable as an input for decision making.

TAKE ACTION: SOCIAL RATINGS

Nielsen data continues to be an important source for media buying decision makers; however, it does not have to be a single source. Summarized in the following list are three key ways to take advantage of the insights that social media can generate to benefit your media planning and buying strategies.

1. *Take a test drive.* If you are a part of an advertising agency that does not yet have access to Bluefin, Trendrr, or SocialGuide, you are missing out on a wealth of information that can help you and your clients. One of the best ways to get a sense for how each of these tools works—as well as the kind of data they produce— is to give them a try using actual TV campaign examples that you

have running in-market. Each offers different pricing models and, as we illustrated, takes a different approach to social audience measurement.

2. *Conduct experiments.* The list of TV shows where your brand should be (according to social media data) will look different from the list of shows resulting from traditional media planning practices. If a target-appropriate television series bubbles to the top of the social ratings analysis that is low (or nonexistent) on the latter list, conduct a test by placing the TV spot and comparing backchannel chatter across media buys against the different series and networks where your creative is running.

3. *Appraise your social currency.* What are social impressions worth to your brand? In Chapter 1, we described the amplification that can result from these kinds of impressions. We see a promising halo effect that occurs when a brand's nonchoice-based TV spots end up generating lots of positive choice-based social impressions. If these are, indeed, valuable to your brand, you now have another dimension on which to optimize your creative and media buys.

The Data Pool of Social Impressions Is Growing In Both Size and Value

The size of television's collective backchannel is only going to continue to increase as more and more people join and engage on the social networks and services that feed it. As this happens, the data pool by which to measure social TV ratings becomes richer and more representative of the masses. And this, in turn, leads to better insights, which help to produce more resonant content.

Scan for More

Scan this QR code using your mobile device for videos and visuals of the examples and cases referenced throughout this chapter.

Don't have a smartphone with a QR reader app? No problem. You can access companion content directly by going to http://www .socialtvbook.net/tagged/chapter5.

6

Bridge Content

*Driving Engagement
In-Between Episode
Airings*

Television audiences met Southfork Ranch's Ewing family for the first time on Sunday, April 2, 1978 while watching a five-part miniseries called *Dallas* that was broadcast on CBS.[1] In the end, however, there was nothing "mini" about the series; Dallas ended its 357-episode run exactly 13 years, one month, and a day later.

The now-famed TV show dramatized the extravagant, complicated, and shady lives of a fictitious eight-member dynasty who got their wealth from the family oil business started by patriarch John "Jock" Ewing Senior. His eldest son, John "J. R." Ewing Junior—Ewing Oil's hardnosed CEO—quickly became the series' main focal point, and for good reason: His character was brilliantly written in a way such that viewers could not help but love and hate him at the same time.

The end of *Dallas'* second season (or third, if you count the miniseries) would go on to set the stage for a major moment in television history. The episode, entitled "A House Divided," was broadcast on Friday, March 21, 1980—the same day that President Jimmy Carter announced a US boycott of the Moscow Summer Olympics.[2] It soon became clear that the buzz around a fictitious TV narrative would trump a current real-world event among the general public.

In the final 112 seconds of that infamous season finale, audiences find J. R. working late at his office high-rise. Except for the spot illumination of a bankers' desk lamp, it is otherwise quite dark inside. The phone rings: "J. R. Ewing here," he answers—but is met with only silence on the other end. "Hello?" J. R. asks, but hears just two quick clicks, followed by the stark sound of a dial tone.

After about a minute of viewers watching J. R. mull around his office, the camera suddenly fades to black as the ominous sound of footsteps are heard. When the visual returns, TV audiences see the camera panning J. R.'s office suite, as though through the eyes of another individual. The arresting noise of a click and a bump startle J. R. out of a seemingly deep thought. "Who's there?" he abruptly asks. There is no answer.

J. R. hurriedly walks toward the noise's origin, but as he turns the corner into his office's pitch black entryway—"BANG!" A shot is fired as J. R. reels back, grabbing his stomach. "BANG!" A second bullet penetrates him and he doubles over while trying to maintain his balance. He is forced to let go of his grip of the doorjamb and falls to the floor, landing on his back.

The camera quickly zooms into J. R.'s face as he breathes what almost appear to be his last two gasps for air as the episode's background soundtrack reaches a dramatic climax. Bright bold orange letters overlay atop the seemingly lifeless body of J. R.: "Executive Producers PHILIP CAPICE and LEE RICH." The rolling of *Dallas*' familiar closing credits leaves no doubt that season two of the popular television drama has suddenly ended. Viewers are left in complete shock over what just happened on their TV screens.

Not only had *Dallas* redefined the notion of the television "cliffhanger,"[3] it had also triggered a pop culture firestorm as people around the world obsessively began to wonder who shot J. R. And they would have to wait a bit longer than originally expected to find out; a Screen Actors Guild (SAG) strike during the summer of 1980 delayed the start of *Dallas*' third season.[4]

A slew of content in between episode airings further fueled audience curiosity, which was a publicity dream for CBS and their hit show. T-shirts and other memorabilia asking, "Who shot J. R.?" were mass-produced. The July 14, 1980 issue of *People* magazine reported that J. R. bumper stickers outnumbered those of the Carter and Reagan presidential campaigns that were simultaneously taking place.[5] A front cover feature in the August 11, 1980 issue of *Time* headlined, "TV's Dallas: Whodunit?"[6]

At last, during the fourth episode of *Dallas*' third season, incredibly eager audiences around the world had their answer.

An estimated 83 million Americans tuned in to the "Who Done It?" episode—an audience amount just shy of the total voter turnout for the 1980 presidential election, which also took place in November, just 17 days prior to the show's premiere.[7]

Today, that episode of *Dallas* ranks as the number three highest rated television event in history following Super Bowl XLIV and the *M*A*S*H* series finale.[8] Friday, November 21, 1980 will forever be remembered as the day 350 million people worldwide found out "who shot J. R."

Content Turns the Wait in between Episodes into Share-Worthy Anticipation

The far more interesting story about the *Dallas* murder-attempt mystery is not the fact that Kristin Shepard (the vengeful younger sister of J. R. Ewing's wife) was eventually revealed as the anonymous gunman. Rather, it was the way in which content helped TV viewers build excitement in between episodes.

This is what we refer to as "bridge" content, and it is the fuel that is pumped to loyal television series' fans in-between broadcast episode airings keeping the TV show top-of-mind and buzzed about. Bridge content energizes its viewers, helps spread the word, and aims to increase program tune-in as a result. While clothing, buttons, mugs, and magazines were used as bridge content for *Dallas* during the summer of 1980,[9] TV networks today have the Web—along with the publishing, distribution, and amplification power of social media.

A research study of over 1,500 TVGuide.com users revealed that, overall, people are more likely to use social media to talk about a television broadcast before and (most heavily) after their favorite TV show airs.[10] This is especially true with serial dramas (like *Dallas*), where television viewers become deeply immersed into the actual broadcast content—and are much more likely to share their feelings at the end of the show versus during.

TV networks that are clued into this pattern are able to add a little "content kick" to the inertia of the organic conversations that are already taking place about their shows. This allows producers, writers, and marketers to help connect the tail of the conversation about the previous episode to the head of the conversation for the upcoming one—thus maintaining (or increasing) overall levels of chatter about their shows.

Facebook Is an Ideal Engagement Platform for a TV Show's Bridge Content

It was reported in May of 2011 that over 275 million people have "liked" at least one TV show on Facebook—totaling well over one and a half billion show "likes" within the social network.[11] Furthermore, 17 of the top "liked" Facebook pages belong to television shows. In case you are wondering, the most liked TV series on Facebook (as of September 2011) is *Family Guy*—with over 35 million likes.[12]

We all know by now why every page owner covets a quality "like" on Facebook. Once someone has liked your page, they have, in essence, signed-up to receive your page's posts within their own newsfeed. You no longer need to worry about a user coming to visit your page; now your content will be delivered directly to them. However, not all people who like your page will see your posts. Actual estimates put the amount of people who ever return to a Facebook page after having "liked" it between only 10 and 12 percent[13]—which makes appearing in users' newsfeeds of paramount importance on Facebook.

But getting Facebook page likes is only half the battle. Only about 3 to 8 percent of a Facebook page's fans (a.k.a. "likes") actually see a given post within their newsfeeds.[14] This has to do with the fact that Facebook gives higher priority to those posts it deems as "top stories" and appear, using an algorithm called EdgeRank that is based on the amount of feedback a post receives.

"Feedback" is expressed as a percentage and is defined by the amount of likes and comments each post receives relative to its page's total fan base. The goal is therefore to create Facebook posts in such a way so that they inherently garner fan responses. The more responses one receives, the better the chance more fans will join—and thus, more people will see your post. This requires that TV networks (and all brands, for that matter) create Facebook posts with content that resonates.

But how do you know whether your brand—or your page—is appealing to your current and potential fans? Facebook page owners are able to monitor, in real-time, the percent feedback a given post currently has. They also have access to more detailed analytics by using Facebook's "Insights" tool that shows and ranks posts by their feedback scores. This allows page owners to see common themes among most and least popular posts; they can then dial up the kind of content that is getting the best feedback, and reduce or eliminate it for posts that are not.

With more than 30 billion pieces of content being shared on Facebook each month,[15] there is a lot of competition for one's newsfeed real estate. Pages that favor acquiring rapid large quantities (versus quality) of likes will suffer from low feedback scores and an overall disengaged social community. Therefore, a TV show's content strategy must include a targeted fan acquisition approach.

TV networks who take the time to do this for their television series pages are able to tap in to the 50 percent of Facebook users who log into the social network every day. Since each user has an average of 130 friends, the bridge content with which they interact has a chance of being shared and amplified organically to their friends.

After all, as Facebook founder Mark Zuckerberg said in May of 2011 during the closing session of the e-G8 Internet Forum in Paris—TV (as well as books and movies) is among the next products to become social through the website.[16]

The CW Wants to Ensure It Offers Their Facebook Fans Value over Volume ▬

Our social media audience is one of our most important marketing tools right now. If we are going to rely on this audience, we need to be very thoughtful with how we treat them. We treat this audience with respect. We're not going to be blasting messages to them fifty-two weeks out of the year. If we don't have something valuable to say, we're not going [to] waste their time and clog up their newsfeeds.

—Alison Tarrant, EVP Integrated Sales and Marketing at The CW

The Vampire Diaries debuted on The CW television network on September 10, 2009. Based on the novels written by L. J. Smith, the TV series centers on two vampire brothers, Damon and Stefan Salvatore, who both fall for the same high school girl, Elena Gilbert, upon returning to their hometown of Mystic Falls, Virginia. The show's plot carries an added twist in that the brothers found themselves in a similar love triangle back in the nineteenth century with a merciless vampire by the name of Katherine Pierce who bears an unusually striking resemblance to Elena Gilbert.

Currently in its fourth season, *The Vampire Diaries* Facebook page is one of the most vibrant of The CW online communities, with over nine million fans. A new cast photo was displayed on the page three weeks before the show's fourth season premiere—and it received over 36,000 "likes" and 4,000 comments.

This reaction contrasts starkly to the kind of feedback acquired by the posts that were displayed before and after the cast photo—which garnered only one-seventh the amount of fan engagement. It is clear based on this response that *The Vampire Diaries* fans engage the most with exclusive or original content. For instance, a series of candid photos taken from the 2011 Comic-Con received close to 32,000 Facebook likes.

The CW has done a great job of varying the content formats distributed on *The Vampire Diaries* Facebook page. One post featured a custom audio playlist from season three that used streaming music service Spotify. Another post linked directly to iTunes to preview or buy the latest season just released for "catch up" watching. In addition, the network used the "Facebook Questions" feature to post a poll asking fans what their favorite episode was—and there were over 100,000 responses.

ABC's *Modern Family* Involves Fans by Asking Their Opinions

As a way to generate awareness for *Modern Family's* special one-hour season three premiere, the show's network, ABC, posted two cast photos that were identical—except for the lead-in copy. They simply asked their over four million fans to vote (but in a clever way): "We need your help! We can't decide which copy line we like better for our latest poster, so we want to know what you think. After all, you do have great taste. Take a look, and vote by commenting or liking the poster with the line you prefer."

One of the poster photos had over 2,600 "likes," while the other had eight times that amount. By merely asking for their opinions, ABC got its fans to generate millions of social impressions promoting *Modern Family*.

Similarly, just before Mother's Day, ABC posted a poll asking *Modern Family* fans which parent is more "motherly" (between Cam and Mitch). Cam won by a long shot, getting over 35,000 votes. Not only was the post timely, but it also played to the spirit and humor of the show and its characters.

To help drive viewers to *Modern Family's* "Boys' Night" episode that premiered on March 23, 2011, ABC took a simple, built-in Facebook feature and added a little creative twist, thereby making a much more substantial effect. When the character Jay realizes during the episode that his wife Gloria and her son Manny are taking him to the symphony instead of seeing a Frankie Valli concert, he parts ways with them and coincidentally ends up at the same bar where his son Mitchell is having dinner with his partner Cam and their three friends.

Since the focal point of the show centered on the dinner at the restaurant, ABC created a Facebook event and, essentially, invited fans to have dinner with the group on the day and at the time the episode premiered. The event was titled "Boys' Night with Cam, Mitch, Pepper, Longinus . . . and Jay"; and its invitation yielded a little over 4,000 RSVPs. Not only did each RVSP show up in friends' Facebook newsfeeds; it also acted literally as a calendar reminder to tune in live to watch the episode.

CBS Takes Content from *How I Met Your Mother* to a New Level

Over 18 million people "like" *How I Met Your Mother* on Facebook, and CBS does a nice job of integrating a healthy serving of behind-the-scenes bridge content to pique curiosity about upcoming episodes. The network's Facebook post announcing that the show had been renewed for another two years generated over 42,000 likes.

One of the things that *How I Met Your Mother*'s loyal fans and insiders like best about this show is its "in-character" Web content. When a website or Web content is mentioned on-air, it is a pretty safe bet that it has actually been created for fans to discover and explore.

For example, in season three's "Everything Must Go" episode, Lily and her fiancé Marshall owe money for costly, but necessary, home improvements. In desperate need of quick cash, Marshall's solution is to create a website to sell Lily's expensive clothes. Not only does the site mentioned in the show, LilyAndMarshallSellTheirStuff.com, actually exist; it also acted as a real live auction featuring items from the show that were sold to help raise money for Children's Hospital Los Angeles.[17]

How I Met Your Mother is a bridge content machine. The fictitious bank where playboy Barney Stinson works has a real website at GoliathBank.com. In addition, fans can actually purchase Barney's "Bro Code" book, watch his video resume, and read his blog, which is simply called "Barney's Blog" and kept up-to-date with regular entries by "Barney."

Early in the second season, it was hilariously revealed that the character Robin Scherbatsky had a teen career as a pop artist when she lived in Canada and was known as "Robin Sparkles." Back in 2006 when the episode aired, it mentioned that a music video of her had been posted to MySpace; of course, CBS created an actual MySpace page for it, complete with the music video. Today, the official Robin Sparkles Facebook page has over 100,000 fans.

While all of this fictitious yet real bridge content exists in various places online, CBS uses the *How I Met Your Mother* Facebook page as a means to tie much of it together—thus increasing its discoverability. Since a good portion of the content posted on the Facebook page physically lives on CBS.com, the website benefits from a healthy dose of referral traffic, thanks to an ever-growing and active Facebook population.

Not All Bridge Content Is Delivered via Facebook

Ultimately, we are a content company. It's not about technology gimmicks; instead, it's about creating great content with which people want to engage. While we execute in a way that's based on our viewers' evolving digital behaviors, it all comes back to having great content as a starting point.

— Jacob Shwirtz, Director of Social Viewing at
Viacom Media Networks

The Canada-born *Degrassi* franchise began in 1980 with 26 episodes of *The Kids of Degrassi St.* It became *Degrassi Junior High* in 1987, with three seasons airing in the United States on PBS.[18] Known for tackling tough and often controversial teen issues, the series gives its viewers a birds'-eye look at students attending a fictional school in Toronto. *Degrassi Junior High* was renamed to

Degrassi High in 1989 as the series storyline took the cast into high school.[19] Together there were a total of 96 episodes from when the original series aired and its final broadcast on February 11, 1991.

Following a Canadian TV movie in 1992 titled *School's Out*, the Degrassi franchise was revived in 2001 with *Degrassi: The Next Generation*. The new series (currently in its eleventh season) picks up with the teen children of the original *Degrassi High* characters and maintains the original series' dramatic and topical issues-oriented spirit. Shortened to just *Degrassi* going into its tenth season, the show is broadcast in the United States on TeenNick (part of MTV Networks).[20]

The network has done a thorough and innovative job of using the Web to build a cross-platform dramatic storytelling universe for *Degrassi* that is filled with bridge content for the show's fans to snack on while waiting for the next broadcast episode. Over the past two seasons, 24 of *Degrassi*'s characters have been brought to life on Twitter through a collaboration between *Degrassi* series' writers and Nickelodeon's digital marketing team. This endeavor was the first of its kind in interactive and cross-platform dramatic storytelling, and it allows fans to follow any of their favorite characters to get a peek of what goes on in between (and during) *Degrassi* episodes. An aggregated tweet stream of all of the show's characters, called "Degrassi DL," lives on the *Degrassi* show pages on TeenNick.com. Additionally, Facebook provides an interconnected view of the characters' Twitter narrative.

The most compelling part of TeenNick's *Degrassi* bridge content strategy is how the network uses its characters' Twitter accounts to converge its online properties. On August 30, 2011, the morning of the *Degrassi* graduation episode premiere, Chantay Black's character (known as the school's gossip queen) tweeted "it's graduation day!!! Remember when we just started at Degrassi? #nostalgic http://ow.ly/6gssV." The hyperlink that "Chantay" included leads people to a specific post on the Degrassi Daily Gossip Tumblr blog. The post showcases a photomontage of Chantay from over the years, and helped to get viewers even more excited about the upcoming episode. The Degrassi Daily Tumblr blog is another platform that the series' producers utilize to enrich both the broadcast and online storytelling experience. The Twitter and Tumblr accounts work in tandem to create a multidimensional online *Degrassi* universe that provided new content daily—including photos and quotes from the characters' perspective.

Most of the Degrassi characters' Twitter profiles—who also tweet during the on-air broadcasts—have at least 5,000 followers; several have double that amount. One character, Elijah Goldsworthy, who tweets under @RealEli, has close to 16,000 followers. He is, apparently, one of the more popular characters on the show.

Bridge content is a vehicle that extends a television storyline beyond the boundaries of its broadcast airing. Jacob Shwirtz, Viacom Media Network's Director of Social Viewing, sees social media as a catalyst that opens up creative possibilities and fosters cross-team collaboration:

> Social TV breaks down the barriers between the TV people and the marketing people who are working much more collaboratively with show producers, creators, and talent. Consumers and fans have a growing desire to be a part of the show every single step of the way. They expect to be able to have their voice heard on everything; not just after the show has been edited and put online, but starting even earlier. The closer that digital folks and linear TV folks start to work, the cooler the experiences we'll be able to create.

Television networks like TeenNick are increasingly using social media to put new twists on their digital content. However, the idea of bridge content has been around for quite some time.

Sci-Fi Used Bridge Content in 2006 to Connect Two Television Seasons

The 1978 dramatic outer space science fiction series *Battlestar Galactica* was updated and aired as a two-part three-hour miniseries in December of 2003. Because it was SyFy's third most-watched program ever,[21] the network developed it into a full-fledged television series that premiered on October 18, 2004.[22]

Battlestar Galactica's second season ended as an abrupt cliffhanger in which the main characters' new home planet had just been discovered and taken over by the very arch enemy (the Cylons) from whom they had been running and hiding. This, of course, left show viewers with a bit of angst having to wait seven months for the new season premiere's plot resolution.

In order to satisfy anxious *Battlestar Galactica* fans' appetites, the network released a 10-part Web series of short (under five minutes) online videos one month before its season three premiere.[23] Two "webisodes" per week were posted on SciFi.com, YouTube, and iTunes. The serial bridge content helped to fill in the gap of events where season two dramatically left off and where season three picks back up.

While many TV networks have produced online companion content for their TV shows for years, advances in technology—along with growing social media and mobile adoption—continue to pave new ways for people to experience and share that content.

Bravo's Bridge Content Influences Its On-Air Content

In the old days, it was all about digital extensions. We don't want to be an extension. We want to be a digital experience that helps drive overall viewing, whatever the platform, where the digital series is just as critical as the show.
—Lisa Hsia, Executive Vice President of Digital Media at Bravo

The first season of Bravo's *Top Chef* made its debut on March 8, 2006.[24] The reality show uses a competition format to feature aspiring chefs who perform various cooking-related challenges. Their culinary results are then judged by a panel of four renowned food and restaurant industry professionals. Over the course of the season, contestants are eliminated until only one is declared the "Top Chef."

The show's ninth season premiered in November of 2011 and included a major new "transmedia" twist. A parallel web video series, appropriately called *Top Chef: Last Chance Kitchen*, gave eliminated contestants a second chance to get back onto the show. Hosted by lead judge Tom Colicchio, each week's eliminated contestant from the TV series competed against the previous week's winner of the Web series. The remaining two *Last Chance Kitchen* contestants went head-to-head to qualify for the on-air *Top Chef* finale.

The Web series marked the first time that Bravo's digital content affected its on-air show content. This was a brilliant move on the network's part to use the concept of bridge content to help drive the TV show. Fans of *Top Chef* who truly wanted to be "in the know" needed to watch both the TV show and the Web series in order to see who might be coming back to compete in the season finale.

Bravo has demonstrated a consistently curious and determined "test and learn" approach over the years when it comes to social TV. As the network's Executive Vice President of Digital Media, Lisa Hsia, said to us:

> When you're innovating, there is no template. I would describe social TV as we know it today as still in the caveman era. You have a rock and you're trying to make it into an arrowhead, or a bowl, or mortar and pestle. I don't think we're yet able to say what works or what doesn't. I think it's really about understanding what the various components are and how users are responding to them, and then evolving the experience around that.

Bravo's *Top Chef* transmedia play allowed the network to elevate its Web bridge content to a similar "premium" status as the TV show itself. Most likely, this is just the beginning.

NBC Is Baking Digital Components into Its TV Shows from the Onset

We don't necessarily think of it as bridge content; it's the core of what we do at NBC.com. We take what's on air for 30 or 60 minutes and we continue that storyline online. We try to create additional experiences and fan engagement online so that when the show is not on-air the users can remain as interested—if not more so—in the show.

—Dana Robinson, Senior Director of Social Media at NBC.com

Top-rated entertainment website NBC.com [25] is jam-packed with Web content in just about every size, shape, and flavor across the broadcast network's television series. From social games and quizzes to exclusive webisodes and video mash-ups, NBC approaches its online content and properties as a key component to its overall content strategy. And there literally is something for *everyone* within the NBC.com Web ecosystem.

Since November of 2006, the site has been showcasing a segment called "Ask Tina" during which viewer questions for *30 Rock's* Tina Fey are collected from the show's message board, Facebook page, and Twitter. Every so often—maybe about once per month—Tina is informally captured on video answering a few of the more stand-out questions. The comedic actress started doing this from the show's infancy and there are now over 40 "Ask Tina" videos on NBC.com.

Questions have ranged from series-related insights to asking what Tina's superpower is (her answer, incidentally, is, "I can be as mean as a tornado in one second"). Tina layers her off-the-cuff comedic flair on the answers, making for low-cost, simple-to-produce, yet extremely funny and compelling bridge content. Not only does it energize loyal fans and make them feel closer to the show; it also inspires them to want to share and, hence, generate social impressions.

While "Ask Tina" works well for *30 Rock*, there is not a one size fits all bridge content formula germane to all NBC shows—or programs from any network, for that matter. Since each show is very different, it would not make sense to treat it according to some kind of standardized template. However, there is one thing that is common across NBC's digital executions, as NBC.com's Senior Director of Social Media Dana Robinson shared with us:

> Different genres play to different strengths. Reality shows allow you to work directly with the contestants, because they are real people who are using social media, just like the viewers. With scripted shows, we find the webisodes, highlights and viral mash-ups continue to be popular. We try different things for different genres of shows, but ongoing community management is the common thread that ties everything together. Once you've brought loyal fans to the table, nurturing them and keeping them around as evangelists for the shows is critical. Fans tend to feel a little more important and respected when they know they are talking to somebody; we want them to feel like they're engaging with real people and not just a giant TV network.

NBC recognized early on in the process how vital it was to give content to fans that they could discuss when their favorite shows were off the air, during hiatus, or in-between seasons. An original Web series in 2006 for *The Office* featured show characters who ordinarily did not get a lot of TV airtime. "The Accountants" was a big success for NBC.com, due in large part to the collaboration between the online team, the show's writers, and producers. The network has worked over the years to scale this collaboration to the present day.

The Office's most recent Web series was born out of a season seven episode mention of characters Kelly and Erin's girl band. The online videos tell the story of the faux musical group Subtle Sexuality as they film their very first music video, "Male Prima Donna." Their second song and video, "Girl Next Door," debuted on SubtleSexuality.com in the spring of 2011. An entire in-character Web universe was created around the band—including a fan club, tour schedule, and the ability to buy real Subtle Sexuality concert t-shirts.

Bridge content is no longer just an afterthought that gets tacked on after a show has been created. In fact, the label "bridge content" may have an almost demeaning, second-rate connotation at this point. It is an exciting element of the future of television, as viewers increasingly get to experience rich content that is much more editorially woven together, or complementary to the show's storylines (across media channels) that endure well beyond the confines of a show's broadcast airtime.

Yes, Even *Sesame Street* Is Doing It

The *Sesame Street* YouTube channel has garnered close to 200,000 subscribers since its creation in 2006. The library of videos contains over 1,000 vintage clips from the educational children's show from over the years that have collectively received over 500 million views. The folks at *Sesame Street* have also included several more recent pop culture spoofs that virally spread like wildfire.

Their most popular spoof was on the now-infamous February 2010 Old Spice "The Man Your Man Could Smell Like" campaign. However, *Sesame Street*'s version featured furry blue monster Grover assuming the role of actor Isaiah Mustafa. While Old Spice was promoting shower gel in its commercial, *Sesame Street* was demonstrating the word "on." As the video progresses to the humorous "I am on a horse" reveal that takes place at the end of the original Old Spice ad, viewers find Grover riding "on" a cow instead. *Sesame Street*'s "Smell Like a Monster" video was posted to YouTube on October 6, 2010, and has amassed over eight million views.

Some of the other *Sesame Street* TV-related spoofs available on YouTube include "30 Rocks," "Desperate Houseplants," and "True Mud."[26] They also did one about *Mad Men* called the same, which had a puppet of Don Draper from the AMC series expressing his anger because he is "mad." That video has been viewed about a million times so far.

Although the YouTube *Sesame Street* content does not specifically or directly bridge any two of the show's episodes or seasons, it does reignite top-of-mind awareness and nostalgia for the long-running PBS series among adults who may then tune in with their children more frequently—or at the very least, help to spread the funny content they saw.

Advertiser Sponsorships Help Monetize Television Bridge Content

All of the "Ask Tina" videos on NBC.com are preceded by a 15-second video ad. While preroll is one way to align your brand to bridge content, there are additional methods to execute integrated sponsorships—approaches that just might increase consumer receptivity to your message.

Networks like NBC work hard to create brand integrations that feel organic. For instance, *The Biggest Loser*'s online community hosts a food journal section where members can blog about what they are eating. This section of the site has been sponsored by brands related to eating healthier, such as Milk, Extra, and General Mills.

The Degrassi DL bridge content referenced earlier is "brought to you by" a major feminine hygiene brand. The brand's logo not only appears on the aggregated tweet stream creative but also embeds its brand message into the actual Twitter conversation as a sort of "commercial break" using a branded hashtag.

The *Top Chef: Last Chance Kitchen* Web series was sponsored exclusively by Toyota. Similarly, when The CW wanted to do something special for its *Vampire Diaries* Facebook fans, Ford funded the production of an exclusive video series that featured the show's producers (Kevin Williamson and Julie Plec) answering fan questions. Ford branding was included in the messaging around the "Inside the Vampire Diaries" video series but more powerfully, as branded content itself.

Show actress Candice Accola, who hosted the series, kicked off each webisode by engaging with the 2011 Ford Fiesta. While it may sound like blatant product placement, its execution was much more naturally built in to the bridge content's narrative storyline. For instance, in one of the videos, Candice meets Executive Producer Julie Plec to ask her questions from Facebook fans. Along the way to the studio, she stops at a cupcake shop to get a treat to bring Julie. To get there, she is shown driving the Ford Fiesta in which she makes a hands-free call to get directions. This, of course, naturally showcases some of the car's features—but in a more indirect way.[27]

However, embedding one's brand into network TV's online extensions is not the only way for advertisers to use bridge content to reach their target audience. They can also create their own.

TV Commercials Have Experimented with Their Own Bridge Content

In February of 2010, Toyota launched a campaign for the all-new Sienna minivan. The series of TV spots depicted a very relatable and somewhat quirky family of four: Two parents with two very young kids (a girl and a boy). Delivered in an almost *Modern Family*/*The Office* sitcom-style format, the series of TV commercials are funny and resonant by themselves. But sometimes more is better, as Toyota decided to give viewers of the spots additional content with the hope of extending their receptivity and driving choice-based and social impressions.

The end of each of the Sienna commercials includes the voiceover, "Meet the family and the new Sienna on YouTube," accompanied by a lower third displaying the URL, "youtube.com/sienna." Toyota clearly understood the difference between its TV audience and the YouTube audience, as online visitors were shown a hilarious two-minute, 36-second "Swagger Waggon" music video.

In what is a prime example of content-as-advertising, the Sienna parents are lip-syncing a relatively heavy rap song with the lyrics, "Where my kids at?" The online video is not only extremely funny because of its surprising juxtaposition; it also naturally compels viewers to want to share it. And share it they did, as "Swagger Waggon" currently has close to 10 million views on YouTube.

Bridge content for TV commercials allows advertisers to push their boundaries a little bit and produce hard working (yet still brand-appropriate) stories that would not ordinarily air as a 30-second television spot. This bridge content does not have to necessarily be an off-the-wall comedic video; it could instead take the form of an extended storyline.

Purina's Fancy Feast took the latter approach with its "Storybook Wedding Commercial" that aired starting in August of 2011. This was a continuation of the brand's successful "Engagement" ad that ran six months prior featuring a white fluffy kitten wearing a "Will you marry me?" medallion.

For the wedding ads, however, the brand opted to end their TV spot with a set of art cards that prominently read, "There's much more to this love story. Watch now on YouTube." Those viewers who executed their "choice-based impression" were welcomed with an extended three-minute version of the wedding TV spot that resolved its emotional cliffhanger and, of course, had a tear-producing happy ending.

Together, the Toyota and Purina examples illustrate that bridge content does not discriminate against genres. Whether comedy or drama, what gave these brands success was not merely the tactic of bridge content. It was the actual resonant content in the TV spot *itself* that left people craving more. A bridge content strategy will not work if it does not springboard off of great content in addition to being great content.

TAKE ACTION: BRIDGE CONTENT

Television bridge content can be a powerful place for advertisers to embed their brands to reach an inherently engaged audience. The following are three ways to maximize the receptivity of your brand message using bridge content.

1. *Span screens.* Bridge content provides a unique opportunity to continue the story and thus, your brand sponsorship. Carry over your broadcast TV series integration into the show's corresponding bridge content in order to reinforce and connect your brand message across media channels.
2. *Become part of the story.* People engage with bridge content because of the *content*—not the advertising. So find ways to integrate your brand message into the storyline or context of the content in order to drive both brand receptivity and resonance.
3. *Push for innovation.* The most exciting part about content is its complete lack of creative boundaries. When sponsoring a TV show's bridge content, partner with the television network to *collaboratively* create an innovative experience that energizes the audience who engages with it.

Remember That Bridge Content Is Choice-Based

The phrase "bridge content" might sound a bit second-class, but that could not be further from the truth. The coveted value of this kind of content is due to the choice-based impressions that result from audiences *choosing* to engage with it. This is valuable to both television networks and advertisers. As more "transmedia" type of content is created, there will be greater (and more creative) opportunities for brands to impact target audiences.

Scan for More

Scan this QR code using your mobile device for videos and visuals of the examples and cases referenced throughout this chapter.

Don't have a smartphone with a QR reader app? No problem. You can access companion content directly by going to http://www .socialtvbook.net/tagged/chapter6.

7

Audience Addressability

Using Online and Direct Mail Targeting Practices on TV

American electronics giant RCA–owned W2XBS was 1 of 10 stations issued a commercial television license by the FCC on May 2, 1941. Two months later, on July 1, 1941, it became the first television station to begin commercial broadcasting under the new call letters WNBT. Though these call letters have changed a few times over the years, they are known today as New York City's familiar WNBC.[1]

"America runs on Bulova time" was the tagline heard by fans who tuned into a Dodgers versus Phillies baseball game over 70 years ago. The famous watchmaker paid only nine dollars to run its brand's television commercial to a broadcast audience. Their 10-second TV spot simply showed a clock superimposed over a map of the United States.[2]

For decades, brands could pretty much guarantee that every viewer would see the exact same TV spot during each commercial break when they bought broadcast media in a local market or on a national network. While television has the benefit over other mediums of enabling advertisers to reach mass audiences with a consistent message, this form of advertising also comes with its share of inherent waste.

The advent of online advertising, where targeting and optimization are fundamentally built into the medium, has put pressure on the television industry to become more than just a mass medium and to instead incorporate the targeting and real-time ad serving capabilities that the Internet boasts. Add to that various addressable television technologies and targeting built on a direct mail model, and you have the ability to precisely pursue the consumers who are most likely to buy your products on a mass scale. The integration of these technologies presents marketers with the potential for a very powerful opportunity.

We have attempted throughout this book to prove why television is far from dead. One of the many challenges that the 70-year old medium faces today is the perception that it does not have the same level of targeting and accountability as other channels of media. However, as we discuss in this chapter, the advent of the digital set-top box and the data it can now provide—coupled with traditional direct marketing databases, such as Experian or Axciom—has given television the potential to reduce wasted impressions and become a more accountable advertising platform.

Addressable Television Advertising Promises High-Impact, Yet Precise, Television Spots

Addressable TV advertising brings together the power of video storytelling and efficient audience reach of TV, along with the targeting of direct mail and measurability of Internet advertising. For TV operators and networks, addressable TV ads offer a more efficient and precise means to promoting products, services, and programs. Agencies gain the opportunity to create more meaningful and relevant ads. Advertisers benefit from the ability to optimize messaging and reduce waste. And consumers benefit from seeing ads that are more engaging and meaningful.
　　—Claudio Marcus, Executive Vice President at Visible World

Marketers have long hoped for a day when they can stop sending ads out to the entire television universe, and instead target TV commercials for specific products only to those people who are in the market for those goods. Dog owners would get dog food commercials, families with babies would get diaper ads, and people suffering from high blood pressure would get messages about hypertension drugs. While this form of addressability is already possible today, we are still in the infancy stages of its true potential.

The concept of addressable television ads has been proclaimed for years as the Holy Grail of advertising. And why not? Television's greatest strength is its ability to deliver large-scale audiences. Providing a method to send ads to smaller, more niche groups of consumers who are more likely to be interested in the product or service being promoted should drive all brand and sales metrics for advertisers.

Nowadays, the technology embedded in digital set-top boxes has paved the way for television advertising to behave more like online advertising or direct mail. What those two mediums have done that television has not been able to do—until recently, that is—is to aim messages more precisely to viewers, thus enabling greater relevancy.

You may have noticed from what you have read so far that every chapter in our book has started the same way—with an opening anecdote that describes the consumer's use of a new technology, or an explanation of how a consumer could have used a technology had it been available during previous historic television events. This chapter is different in that the topic it covers—addressable advertising—does not require consumers to change their behavior. The change must instead occur in cable operator technology and media sales business models. The end goal is still a modification of consumer behavior—specifically, a greater likelihood that consumers will pay more attention to television ads since they are now much more relevant to them.

While we all agree the potential in this area is great, several major issues have slowed the rollout of addressable advertising. There are privacy issues, technology issues, business model challenges, cost implications to the advertiser for increased creative development and media buy premiums. Additionally, the plan and buy management software systems like Donovan, Mediabank, and Strata that agencies use to electronically track inventory purchased have yet to develop applications that allow them to manage this inventory in a similar fashion as other media buys.

Addressability from the Marketer's Perspective Is About Targeting

The first step toward addressability requires that marketers identify their target segment profiles. It is important that these profiles are clearly defined and distinct from one another. Technology companies like Visible World and INVIDI have developed software that enables a cable multiservice operator (MSO) or satellite provider to identify the set-top box for the target profile. The subscriber files for the profile generated with the software are provided to a trusted third party, like Experian or Axciom, which then uses the files to make a blind match of the household data in the subscriber file with its marketing and transactional database.

Advertisers interested in conducting an addressable TV ad campaign are then able to use the trusted third party's vast consumer information database to determine counts of select consumer households based on a variety of predefined criteria. Advertisers can also overlay their own customer files with their related attributes to the third-party file to make the database even richer. After they combine this data, the marketer has a database for the segmentation. Once advertisers select sets of consumers based on a match to a defined set of criteria, these segments are represented as sets of households. Each one has unique household identifiers that advertisers can target with specific customized TV ads.

Messaging then needs to be created for each of the segments. For example, let's say that an advertiser is trying to reach a multiethnic audience. They may create one ad for the African American segment, one for the Hispanic segment, one for the Asian segment, and one for the Anglo segment. Most addressable ad campaigns have two to five messages. There are currently bandwidth issues with sending more than five messages; however, it is expected that these limitations will decrease over time, thereby allowing even more precise segmentation.

Addressability from the Cable Operator Perspective Is About Inventory and Logistics

A cable television network like Discovery or ESPN sells most of the ads within their broadcast inventory. However, the cable operator is given two minutes per hour to sell local ads. Cable operators can then allocate this inventory as either a general market ad *or* an addressable ad. So how does the cable operator know when to insert the ad? There is a special cue, a subaudible tone that is inserted into the broadcast stream by the cable network at the time when the local advertising opportunity comes up. The cable operator has equipment that recognizes the cue tone and goes off to an ad server that determines which ad to show.

Once an advertiser purchases the addressable inventory from a cable system, satellite provider, telco, or cable network, software developed by Visible World or INVIDI intersects the video stream from the cable operator at just the right time to introduce the targeted ad. What happens next is a "seamless switch" that takes the viewer from one stream of content to a different one—essentially, from one channel to another channel. At the end of delivering the addressable content to the viewer, the viewer is switched back to the original channel. The TV viewer doesn't perceive any of this switching, and has no idea this is happening. It is a completely smooth process.

There Are Challenges Slowing the Adoption of Addressable Advertising

The advances in digital set-top box are what made Addressable TV advertising possible. This piece of equipment has digital identifiers that allow households to be profiled. And along with this ability also comes one of the major challenges slowing the rollout of addressable TV: privacy.

Privacy Is a Major Concern with Addressable Advertising

Consumer advocacy groups have raised privacy concerns over the data that has been collected and used to enable addressable television advertising. The television industry has paid close attention to carefully manage actual or perceived risks, and has taken an approach to addressable advertising that is more similar to direct mail than the Web. As just discussed, cable operators are part-nering with trusted third-party data providers such as Experian (mentioned earlier) to create a "blind-match" approach where no personal identifiable consumer or viewer information (PII) is exchanged with advertisers. Technology companies such as Visible World and INVIDI—who have led the opportunity to gather the subscriber data for their MSO and satellite provider clients—have also designed their systems in a way that allows advertisers to col-lect and share this data without compromising personal privacy issues. Once advertisers select sets of consumers based on a match to a defined group of criteria, these segments are represented as sets of households. Each one has unique household identifiers and will be targeted with specific customized TV ads.

"Cable operators have been extremely sensitive to consumer pri-vacy concerns," says Visible World's Marketing EVP, Claudio Marcus. He believes that the addressable TV system that has been put into operation can work *without* the need for cable operators or third-party data providers to reveal any PII to advertisers. He explains, "As it's been implemented, household addressable TV advertising is more akin with how direct mail works today than the more controversial behavioral targeting associated with the Internet."

Technology Challenges Are Starting to Ease

The second major challenge in adopting addressable television advertising is how quickly MSOs can deploy the technology needed to manage addressable ads. This is a space where advertiser inter-est will most certainly drive change at the MSOs and television networks. Marcus believes that many advertisers are still hesi-tant to play in this space until there is sufficient scale, and until operators and networks have demonstrated their commitment to deployment based on advertiser demand. Advertisers can, how-ever, drive more rapid use by encouraging cable operators to adopt this technology. Therefore, Marcus is optimistic, noting that "get-ting involved in addressable TV campaigns signals to both the operators and the networks that advertisers are interested and want more of this."

A key challenge in deploying this technology has come from the set-top box. Because there was a myriad of different set-top boxes— operated by different manufacturers and different operating systems— the industry developed technology to homogenize the environment to a common interface standard known as Enhanced TV Binary Interchange Format (or EBIF for short). EBIF enables proper communication between the application inputs and the system requirements on the operator side. From a practical standpoint, EBIF enables cable providers to deploy addressable and interactive applications on a much larger population of heterogeneous set-top boxes.

Cablevision was the first MSO to have addressability installed across its full footprint; they have a homogenous set-top box environment, and 98 percent of their boxes are manufactured by Scientific Atlanta—all of which are digital. Time Warner, Comcast, and others have grown through acquisition and thus have a more diverse set-top box environment. However, they are aggressively deploying EBIF to enable the use of addressable and interactive applications.

Should the Business Model for Selling Ads Change?

A third challenge is the current business model. The way things presently work, MSOs and cable networks sell inventory that cover either the entire country or an entire market. Each individual commercial unit is owned entirely by one advertiser. Addressable platforms allow advertisers to target specific regions, zones, and even individual households that they believe are more likely to buy their products and services. Thus, their ad buy will cover much less than 100 percent of US television households, thereby enabling them to reduce wasted spending. This sounds great for the advertiser, but it creates challenges on the sales side.

Let's say, for example, that a brand's addressable ad buy covered 25 percent of the country. The seller would then take the remaining three-quarters of the household universe and offer three additional spots for sale. This requires that MSOs and networks be able to sell that remaining inventory to other advertisers. As a result, they will need additional manpower and systems to handle these units—and it is difficult to administer real-time management tools to assign remnant inventory. Networks and other distributors are concerned that they do not yet know how to fully monetize inventory under this model. As former Canoe Ventures CEO David Verklin noted in a 2010 *ADWEEK* article, "Programming networks have made a lot of money on waste. And they have to be convinced that they can make as much or more on efficiency."[3]

Will the cost advertisers incur to run addressable ads justify the increased workload necessary to manage it and compensate for any remnant inventory left unsold? There is money being spent at the system level, by the broadcaster, and by agency at the desktop level. Broadcasters have to invest in formatting (i.e., EBIF). Sellers (local and national) are justifying cost increases by saying messaging is now more relevant, and that advertisers will see measurable brand lift. What should the cost increase be?

Innovation Seems to Be Coming from Outside the Industry

As to be expected with any mature industry like television, advances in technology and business models often come from innovators *outside* the industry. Two such innovation leaders have been Visible World and INVIDI. We have also seen significant development in the cable operator space, both independently by two major cable operators, Cablevision and Comcast, and through Canoe Ventures, a joint venture of multiple leading MSOs.

Because of the substantial effort and cost involved in developing and bringing this technology to the market, many questions still remain about its viability. "Is it worth the amount of effort, resources, and time that's going to be required to get addressable advertising on a national level to a business as usual scale? The only people who can answer that are the people who spend the money in the first place, the marketers," says Canoe Ventures Chief Product Officer, Arthur Orduna. "If advertisers are willing to spend their dollars on addressable delivery, then it's worth the evolution."

Visible World's Technology Enables the Deployment of Addressable Advertising

Visible World was founded in 1999 with the sole purpose of enabling more relevant advertising on television. Their addressable distribution platform allows media owners to offer advertisers increased consumer relevance and engagement by targeting messages to specific segments—from neighborhood cable zones down to specific household segments.

Visible World is the technology provider that supports the Adtag Adcopy service that the nation's leading multisystem cable providers offer. Adtag allows advertisers to take a single commercial and customize it, thereby making it more relevant to an audience based on a geographic location. For example, a retail store with several locations across a region can "tag" the address or telephone number of each location based on where the segment is shown. Adcopy allows advertisers to simultaneously run different spots within a campaign, across separate zones in a market or region. An auto manufacturer, for instance, can use Adcopy to concurrently show ads for a fuel-efficient sedan in the city, a minivan in the suburbs, and a rugged truck in rural areas.[4]

INVIDI's Technology *Also* Moves Addressable Advertising Capabilities Forward

When I joined the company in 2003, the timeline for full deployment was six years—that would take us to 2009. Well we're in 2011 and we're at about one third of households in America. Everyone on

the marketer/agency side wants addressability to work, because it cuts down the waste inherent in television, increases accountability, makes the medium more effective and is much more trackable.
—Michael Kubin, Executive Vice President at INVIDI

All the challenges we have mentioned so far—privacy, technology, and business models—have slowed the rollout of addressable television.

INVIDI was formed in 2000 in Edmonton, Alberta, based on the idea that the digital set-top box was going to change broadcast television advertising. The organization's goal was to allow the distribution of television spots individually to households based on qualifiers—thus changing television from a "one to many" medium into "one to one." INVIDI's powerful suite of advanced tools enables operators to selectively target television viewers with the same accuracy as direct mail and database marketing—without compromising viewer privacy.[5] In fact, privacy was so important to the company at the outset that according to Michael Kubin, INVIDI's EVP, the name INVIDI means "do not see." As Kubin explains, "Privacy is a sensitive issue and the system was built to respect and protect viewers' privacy."

INVIDI's proprietary technology enables television service providers to simultaneously deliver multiple and distinct commercial messages to different households or individual set-top boxes during a single commercial break. The proprietary technology resides in the set-top box, and makes an educated guess as to whom the viewer is (based on what channels are being watched and remote control behavior). It then decides upon the best spot for that viewer to see.

Of course, INVIDI needed distribution in order for this technology to work. Today, the company has contracts with DISH Network, DirecTV, and Verizon—subscribers that add up to about 40 million households. INVIDI has been distributing successfully through Verizon since 2010 and is just now beginning distribution on Dish and DirecTV set-top boxes. INVIDI hopes to have the technology deployed in 20 million households by the end of 2011.

INVIDI's challenges in striking these deals lie in having to convince two constituencies within the cable operators to adopt the technology. INVIDI acknowledges that they need to convince both the business leaders and the technology guys (whom advertisers need on board to actually *get* the technology into the boxes) that this will work and *not* interfere with the consumer experience—and that has not been an easy task. INVIDI's direct relationship with Motorola has allowed them to put its software into the Motorola manufactured set-top boxes. INVIDI believes that this opportunity will eliminate the need to get the technology guys on board at the cable operators and hopefully accelerate deployment.

Cablevision Is Showing Early Successes with Addressable TV Advertising

Cablevision's approach and market results are incredibly important in this space, since Cablevision represents the first real use case that has enough scale for other companies to extrapolate on their conclusions. Cablevision Marketing utilized addressable advertising to deliver more relevant ads to its subscriber base. In order to measure the effectiveness of the addressable ads versus the general market ads, they conducted post-campaign research.

Cablevision utilized a strict test versus control methodology whereby they established individual test and control groups for each target segment. Test groups received targeted ad copy promoting services they had yet to adopt, while control groups received a more generic default ad. The study examined subscription sales activity within the test and control segments in order to measure the addressable campaign's impact. The results were significant. They showed that the incidence of service upgrades among the addressable segments was consistently higher (by double-digit percentage increases) versus the nonaddressable segments.

Cablevision has also seen success outside of their own marketing efforts. Tests in the wireless, armed services, and travel categories have all returned positive results. Ads to the addressable segments either generated higher acquisition rates or had a more engaged audience (as measured by ad view duration) than nonaddressable ad segments.

Comcast Tests Are Also Showing Promise

Comcast Spotlight, Comcast Corp's ad sales unit, has also completed several tests of technology that delivers different ads to different households. The first two tests—conducted in Huntsville, Alabama, and Baltimore, Maryland—both proved to be about one-third more effective in keeping audiences from tuning out the ads.[6] The tests also suggested that viewers who considered the ads to be directed to them as a specific group of households were also less likely to change channels.

While one-to-one advertising at a household level in television has been tested to some success to date, one-to-few advertising is a space in which many MSOs can readily play. National advertisers can target across Comcast's 25 million subscribers on the zone level, and Comcast is able to identify across their subscriber base zones that index higher against a target than others.

A great example of this is a recent test Comcast conducted with a financial services/credit card company. Advertisers deployed television ad spots in targeted Comcast geographies over a nine-month time span. They chose neighborhoods based on a match of Comcast households to Experian data of household income greater than $130,000 and a FICO score greater than 700 (this is important, as a high FICO score indicates a good credit history). ComScore then determined behavior in the Comcast AD TV neighborhoods and the rest of the United States by using the previous year's identical nine months to account for seasonality, national financial services/credit card advertising, and other baseline factors. They conducted analysis that compared panelists' metrics from the baseline period to the test period.

The pre/post test and control design was developed with com-Score to measure brand performance (as measured by online credit card application rates and online card usage) both in the targeted geography (Test) and a lookalike geography that did not receive the targeted media (Control) and compared the differences pre to post campaign. The results were dramatic. The advertiser saw an incremental 51 percent in average credit card statement balances in the zones that received the targeted ad. Within these same zones, the advertiser saw 13,000 to 20,000 incremental online application submissions.

All of these trials have helped their backers learn a great deal of information about making the ads palatable to consumers. According to Comcast Spotlight vice president of strategic initiatives Andrew Ward, "You need to have a well-defined segment of audience and you need a creative unit that matches up to that well-defined segment" in order to get viewers to respond. And when it comes to consumer privacy, "we need to proceed cautiously."

Is Addressability Possible on a National Scale?

Canoe Ventures was founded in 2008 as a joint venture between the country's top six cable operators including Comcast Corporation, Time Warner Cable, Cox Communications, Charter Communications, Cablevision Systems Corporation, and Brighthouse Networks. The objective was to bring measurability, accountability, and engagement to national television advertising and programming.[7] At its inception, there were four categories of focus: addressability, interactive TV, dynamic advertising insertions within video on demand, and more granular measurement and analytics through set-top box data. However, because privacy challenges and cable's technical heterogeneity are only magnified on a national scale, addressability has become a longer-term objective.

Canoe Ventures has learned how complex it is to deploy advanced television capabilities on a national scale. Managing the workflow process across multiple MSOs is difficult for any advanced service, but especially so for addressability. But Canoe has also focused on acting as an industry advocate, that looks at not just how we execute advanced advertising solutions in cable systems on authorized devices but also how to change the management of advanced advertising within the agency environment, which has been an obstacle in selling advanced ads to media agencies. Canoe's Chief Product Officer, Arthur Orduna, believes that they will realize their opportunity when they "get onto a Donovan or MediaBank desktop. That's when we move from being a test/trial to being part of business as usual." This is what is happening with ITV advertising, and Orduna believes that this is one of the milestones that must be reconciled in order to achieve addressability at scale. "We just have to start doing it iteratively."

So while Cablevision, Comcast, and even the satellite providers have seen some success in the addressable space, the rollout of addressable advertising across a true national footprint has been slower than other television advances. Canoe Ventures and others who started in the addressable television space are shifting gears to focus on other television-related innovations. Interactivity within television ads, as well as dynamic ad insertions within video on demand, both seem to be gaining more traction than addressability. While deploying interactivity at a national broadcast level carries its own set of technical and operational challenges, Canoe and its partners have managed to build a cross-MSO and multiprogrammer platform. This is due partly to the earlier standardization work done by CableLabs and MSO engineers to develop the EBIF specification for interactive television.

Interactive ads start at the broadcast point of origination. The programmer inserts interactive EBIF triggers into the national broadcast stream that gets fed to the cable operator. The EBIF

User Agent in the set-top box receives the triggers and executes the appropriate interactive application, on both commercials and in programming. Canoe has been able to do this successfully on a national scale because of major engineering and operations commitments made by their MSO owners, who have rolled out EBIF to more than 25 million cable households as of today. The MSOs will continue to deploy EBIF to more and more households across their markets, enabling Canoe's ability to offer a platform of growing national scale. Canoe's interactive ads are deployed on a broadcast basis, meaning that the same ad is going to all households, so there are no segmentation and targeting issues. While there are still privacy issues and other technological hurdles that need to be overcome for addressability at national scale, the opportunity to enhance marketing efforts on television with interactive solutions gives agencies and their clients the opportunity to enhance their efforts in the near term.

Dynamic ad insertion within video on demand presents another important near-term strategy. While the lion's share of today's television viewing is within linear broadcast and DVR playback, that situation may change as more programming becomes available on demand. It is possible that the introduction of new advertising inventory within on demand content could ultimately dwarf today's broadcast advertising inventory. The ability to dynamically refresh all of the advertising avails within on demand programming creates an enormous supply of impressions as VOD reaches more scale.

Canoe's Arthur Orduna put it best:

There are different modalities toward addressability, and on demand offers another path. It will allow for the development of cohort characteristics that households share with others so that more relevant advertising may be served. This provides an iterative, measured step toward the enhanced relevance that agencies and advertisers desire to create through addressability in a way that does not involve the technology and policy hurdles of addressability to a particular set-top box. The question is, will this be more valuable, less valuable or equally valuable to the theoretical addressable model in the broadcast world?

The data generated through video on demand usage will also be very valuable, since it can be measured at the set-top box level. This will allow us to begin to gather knowledge about those households and their viewing patterns. Given we are early in the VOD marketplace, now is a great time to test and learn. There are multiple business models in the VOD space and media companies are just beginning to realize how to monetize this audience.

A Number of Questions Remain Unanswered

Many open questions still need to be answered to determine if addressable technologies will succeed in changing the way broadcast television is bought and sold. Is the addressable inventory owner seeing value? Is the marketer buying the addressable inventory also seeing value and coming back to buy more? In essence, are the CPMs more effective? Is the marketer saying, "I would rather spend my next set of dollars with you on an addressable campaign than on a linear broadcast"? Will we reach a point where all television ad campaigns by default need to be addressable?

Advertisers are starting to devise ways to solve some of the issues that addressable technologies raise. Addressable ads may require marketers to pay a premium. There may also be additional costs for increased production, since advertisers will likely have to create a range of commercials for the different audiences they are trying to reach. But there could still be a cost savings if the ability to eliminate waste enables the advertiser to spend less overall, knowing their commercials are reaching the more-likely purchasers of their products.

TAKE ACTION: AUDIENCE ADDRESSABILITY

While challenges persist in this space, it is worth it to jump in on the early days of addressability, interactivity, and dynamic ad insertion within video on demand. The goal in this first phase is to *justify* the premium of addressability as it relates to media costs, creative development, and system implementation. Here are a few thoughts on how to build toward success in this space.

1. *Be smart about which advertisers you approach.* You want to approach brands that have multiple products and therefore more money to spend, versus those with a single product and limited creative budgets. The advertiser must also have the stomach to take a "test and learn" attitude, and must have the demographics in its customer base to justify segmentation.
2. *Segmentation is crucial.* Determine what segments you want to reach and align your messaging with the right targets. This will force media and creative staff to work together, which is a benefit not just for addressability, but for all of the opportunities we discuss in this book.
3. *Data drives success.* Adopt a data-driven mentality and be sure you have the systems in place to measure whether or not your campaign was effective. Create tight coordination with direct marketing channels.

Expect a Learning Curve

All this being said—this space is still new. While there have been many successes to date, media companies are still testing these technologies and it is very possible that things may go awry. So, expect a learning curve. It is important to figure out how to help the television industry build toward these advances. Recognize that the analytics for measuring these advances differs from traditional Nielsen measurement. The new metrics will be set-top box data and may not be comparable to values for other television buys measured on Nielsen ratings. And like all statistical results, the lack of data on a large scale presents opportunities for market inefficiencies that could have an impact on pricing and other related factors.

Scan for More

Scan this QR code using your mobile device for videos and visuals of the examples and cases referenced throughout this chapter.

Don't have a smartphone with a QR reader app? No problem. You can access companion content directly by going to http://www.socialtvbook.net/tagged/chapter7.

8

TV Everywhere

Watching TV Content Whenever and Wherever

Twenty-eight-year-old Chris Brum is a third-grade special education teacher as well as a full-time PhD student at Boston College. His 32-year-old partner, Chris Polous, is the director of sales for a Boston residential real estate agency. The two live together in Dorchester, Massachusetts, and though they each have very different TV watching habits, they do have one important element in common: half of their total TV viewing happens on mobile devices.

Chris Brum watches only about five hours of television per week, well below the US average. Because of his work and school schedule, Chris is often on the go. However, the one device he carries with him at all times no matter where he goes is his iPad. He will take time during study breaks at the library to launch either the ABC, HBO, HGTV, or Netflix applications to catch an episode of one of his favorite shows—including popular programs *True Blood*, *Modern Family*, and *Mad Men*. Chris favors the 30-minute sitcom versus a more immersive and longer drama during these times; it gives him just enough of a mental cool down so that he feels ready to resume hitting the books.

Chris tends to watch television later at night when he is at home. If he happens to be in his living room—or if the couple wants to watch television together (or with friends)—they will turn on their traditional TV set connected to a TiVo box using a DirectTV satellite feed. But being in his living room is not the sole deciding factor whether or not to watch TV on the big screen. There are times when Chris is laying on the couch and decides to watch TV but because he is already using his iPad for Facebook or to check e-mail, he opts to keep his tablet device resting comfortably on his chest to stream a TV episode instead of having to find the remote or get up to turn on the television set.

Of the four streaming apps Chris uses, he frequents HBO Go and Netflix due to the content that they have available at the time he wants to watch. But his favorite application is the ABC Player; it is, as he claims, "very clear and organized." Chris also enjoys using his iPad to watch television in bed by propping it up on a pillow next to him. The device has enabled watching television to be a solitary, portable, and on demand experience for him.

Chris Polous, on the other hand, rarely watches live television. About 20 percent of his TV viewing is recorded on the living room TiVo, and he gets the other 80 percent exclusively from Netflix streaming video. Chris uses an Apple TV device that is connected to his living room television set to watch about half of his Netflix content. Just about all of the video that Chris streams from Netflix is comprised of TV shows—not movies. Chris finds that he watches a total of about 14 hours of television content per week across multiple devices and platforms.

As a realtor, Chris's work schedule is nothing close to ordinary. He is on the road a lot and will often fill any downtime he has by watching TV shows like *Battlestar Galactica*, *Stargate*, and *The Wire* using his mobile device's Netflix. Chris has not used any other full episode player apps; he finds that Netflix meets all of his on-demand needs. He also owns an iPad and prefers watching TV on its bigger screen, but he rarely has it with him on the road, and therefore defaults to next best screen available: his iPhone.

Chris uses the urge to watch "catch-up" TV as an incentive to work out. He actually saves certain TV series that he desperately wants to watch for only those times when he is burning calories on the elliptical machine. This approach has helped Chris to increase the frequency of his cardio routine through his motivation to watch the next episode of his favorite TV show.

Despite their frequent solitary television experiences, Chris and Chris do, indeed, watch their living room TV together; however, they tend to focus on the latest episodes of television series they both enjoy, like *True Blood*. There have been moments, however, where they are both in bed each with their own iPad watching a different TV show and using a different full episode application to do so.

Chris and Chris epitomize the notion of "TV everywhere"—a scenario where television is no longer relegated to a box in one's living room. Television is instead becoming device agnostic and an extremely portable medium that is always accessible at will.

Portable Television Actually Dates Back to Over 50 Years Ago

While the 1960s and 1970s saw a number of smaller and more portable television sets hit the marketplace,[1] it was not until 1982 that people were able to hold and watch TV in the palms of their hands. The Sony Watchman™, powered by a mere set of four AA batteries, weighed just shy of one pound and seven ounces. Its two-inch beveled glass screen was, by all accounts, the very first flat screen television.[2]

Featured in the November 1982 issue of *Popular Science* magazine,[3] the Watchman, as the article depicted, stood out among its "Go-Anywhere TV" competitors. With a sleek aluminum casing and compact design at only one and a quarter inches thick, it fit easily into its owners' pockets.

In addition to the black and white LCD screen, the Watchman's front face included a narrow yet elongated speaker. The upper right corner housed the channel dial with its corresponding tuner display directly to the right of the screen. The back of the device featured a fold-out stand that allowed it to rest atop a horizontal surface like a desk or nightstand. The television's power button, located on the upper right-hand side, included a setting for sound in order to help conserve battery life if the device was not plugged in.

Advertising for the product played up its portability, flat screen, and thin design. "The Skinny Sony" was the bold headline of a print ad that appeared in the June 1983 issue of *Black Enterprise*.[4] The advertisement's copy went on to read:

Other "small" TVs would love to have a body like that, but their picture tubes are just too chubby. On the other hand,

Sony's new flat display picture tube is as flat as a pancake (literally), making Watchman extremely easy to hold when you're watching it. And extremely easy to slip into your pocket when you're not. Watch what you want, whenever you want to watch it, because Watchman is the first really personal TV.

Children were clearly a target for the product, and Sony partnered with General Mills in 1983 for a "Watch 'n Play" Watchman giveaway contest.[5] Game cards were placed inside packages of "Big G" cereals like Lucky Charms, Trix, Cocoa Puffs, and Boo Berry. A weekly 60-second TV spot aired during Saturday morning cartoons; it featured two kids at a breaking news desk explaining the contest and announcing the week's featured picture. If the picture shown matched one's Watch 'n Play cards, they would win one of 1,000 Sony Watchmans.

Over the course of nearly two decades, there were 65 models of the Watchman created until it was discontinued in the year 2000.[6] The national cut-over from over-the-air to digital TV transmissions made receiving a signal on the Watchman impossible without a digital converter box.[7]

As TV Becomes Increasingly Digital, Time-Shifted Viewing Has Increased

The idea of recording television shows is certainly not a new one. People had the ability to delay watching their favorite programs when Video Cassette Recorders (VCRs) started to gain mainstream adoption in the late 1970s.[8] Yet it was not until two decades after that a TV recording device was introduced to the world that would forever alter the face of linear television.

At the Computer Electronics Show (CES) in Las Vegas in January 1999, a little-known company called TiVo unveiled its prototype for a Digital Video Recorder (DVR).[9] But this was by no means a mere antianalog VCR. The company touted the device's ability to pause, rewind, and replay live television, thus empowering TV viewers with a new level of content control.

A rival company called Replay TV came out with a similar announcement at CES; however, TiVo beat them to them to market and shipped its very first production box on Friday, March 31, 1999.[10] Eager consumers could purchase the TiVo set-top box at just under $500 (in addition to a monthly subscription) for its bottom-tier model that stored 14 hours of TV recordings.

An article in the October 2, 1999 edition of the *New York Times* said about TiVo, "Analysts predict that its personal video recorder technology will be part of a new, fast-growing sector of the consumer electronics market."[11] And so it happened. Suddenly, the device that was designed to make TV more interactive also armed millions of Americans with the ability to skip TV commercials.

These days, 40 percent of US households use DVRs—almost triple the penetration from just four years prior.[12] While DVR adoption will continue to grow, there is good news for advertisers. Not only do households with DVRs watch more primetime television than their nonDVR counterparts; they are also not skipping as many commercials as once feared.[13] In fact, according to Nielsen, DVR playback of TV shows within three days of their original airing actually ends up increasing TV commercial ratings by 44 percent.[14]

Video on Demand Lightens the Load on the DVR

Shortly after TiVo went into mass production, Time Warner engaged in a pilot program across three US cities to test a service that would allow cable subscribers the ability to browse and watch a library of video content at will.[15] For the first time since the foreshadowed promises describing the "information super highway" in the early to mid-1990s, it seemed that the ability to rent movies from the couch was about to come to fruition. The July 29 issue of *Forbes* pontificated, "Yet there remains that dream that someday, somehow, video-on-demand will catch on with cable customers."[16]

Thanks to the proliferation of high-speed digital networks, video on demand (VOD) services began rolling out to cable subscribers starting in early 2001.[17] According to media analyst firm MAGNAGLOBAL's VOD Forecast Chart, just over 3,000 homes had video on demand access in 2001. Projections for 2012 are 20 times that. The company predicts that VOD will penetrate about 58 percent of US television households by 2016.

While the availability of television content during the early days of video on demand left a lot to be desired, recent years have told a very different story. On April 27, 2011, Comcast became the first VOD provider to offer on demand content from all four major TV networks. The cable company announced the addition of many popular ABC and Fox TV shows the day after their first-run broadcast airing. As a Comcast spokesperson said in their press release, "Our goal is to deliver customers the best and most-current entertainment choices anytime, anywhere so they can catch up and keep up with their favorite TV shows."[18]

On May 25, 2011, Comcast celebrated another major milestone—it reached 20 billion views of its on demand video content since it launched the service in 2003.[19] Back then, there were only 740 videos compared to the 25,000 video choices Comcast offers in 2011. The most popular on demand TV shows include *South Park*, *Entourage*, and *Sex and the City*.[20] As Comcast put it, "Today, time-shifted viewing is part of everyday mainstream life for most Americans."

The Web Puts a Different Spin on Television

In May of 2006—as a growing number of people tossed their dial-up modems in favor of broadband Internet access—ABC did something unexpected. After striking a deal with iTunes the prior year to make its content available for download and purchase, the television network began to offer full episodes of its popular shows on its website—for free. For the first time, watching TV was no longer an activity that was confined to a physical television set. Millions of Americans could now enjoy their favorite TV shows by streaming them onto their computer screens the day after their original broadcast airing.

The network's online move was met with countless accolades from consumers who felt that ABC truly had their best interests at heart.[21] And in 2007, the network's full episode player was enhanced to allow users to expand it into a full-screen view that made streaming high-definition (HD) TV shows (which ABC added later that same year) easier,[22] thereby providing a far richer "television" experience.

All four major broadcast networks had gotten into the website streaming business by the fall of 2006, although ABC.com remained the most popular at the time.[23] Today, over three-quarters of US adults have watched a TV show online versus their television sets.[24] Loyal fans who cannot watch during the original airtime and forget to set their DVRs have another option to stay current with the series. And watching TV online is the only option for some—a notion of "cord-cutting" that we address in detail in Chapter 9.

TV Networks Band Together to Form Hulu

The advent of premium video service Hulu was announced on March 22, 2007 as a joint venture between NBC Universal and News Corporation[25] (and was additionally joined by Disney/ABC in 2009). Hulu was described at the time as "the largest Internet video distribution network ever assembled with the most sought-after content from television and film." The highly anticipated streaming website launched on March 12, 2008—just shy of the anniversary of its announcement.

Hulu's library boasted full episodes of over 250 television series across 50 broadcast and cable networks at the time of its inception. Nielsen rated it number eight among the top 10 video streaming sites within four months of its launch—a point at which it was generating more than 105 video streams in July of 2008.[26] Two years later, Hulu users were producing two and a half times that amount of streams.[27]

Hulu is able to stream content for free using an ad-supported model that is lighter than the typical television broadcast commercial load. Based on data from Nielsen/IAG, the company has stated that its advertising effectiveness is twice that of broadcast television commercials.[28] Hulu purports the fact that it generates more ad revenue per half hour TV episode than cable and DVR (but not yet broadcast), and that its ability to better target audiences increases relevancy and eliminates wasted impressions.

Members of the industry continue to ponder the amount of advertising available within online television streams. Content providers want to ensure maximum monetization potential, while streaming sites need to grow their engaged users, and therefore remain especially sensitive to drop-off. And while it may seem that the viewers themselves are turned off by heavier ad loads, two different studies toward the end of 2010 actually found that this is not the case.[29]

One study conducted by Turner Broadcasting streamed the same 30-minute sitcom with two different advertising loads. One version had only 90 seconds of ads, while the other had 16 minutes. The network found nominal drop-off with the latter. They repeated the experiment with an hour-long drama and found similar results.[30]

Streaming Content Aggregators Expand On Demand Options (for a Price)

The growth of Netflix and what they did to extend viewership to connected and mobile platforms caused cable operators, satellite providers, and telecommunications companies to realize that tethering their programming to the set-top box in the living room was

starting to feel archaic relative to consumer expectations. That's what helped give birth to the idea of TV Everywhere.
—Will Richmond, Editor and Publisher of *VideoNuze*

Netflix became a household name beginning in 1997 when it launched its DVD rental mail-in service.[31] As the company grew and technology matured, Netflix began to turn some of its attention online by kicking off a rollout of "instant viewing" for a subset of its video content library beginning in 2007.[32]

At first, Netflix's streaming content was limited to only 1,000 movies and TV shows, versus its DVD library of over 70,000 titles. Today, the company offers over fifty times the amount of streaming content. It revealed in November of 2010 that half of all of its video streams are television shows.[33] Shortly thereafter, news broke about Netflix plans to invest in more TV content deals.[34] The company announced a deal with CBS in February of 2011, which rounded its library to include content from all four major television networks.[35]

According to Knowledge Network's "Over-the-Top" TV report published in August of 2011, "The average person age 13–54 is watching about two TV episodes and one movie per week via Netflix."[36] Their study also found that regular Netflix users also watch more television content when measured by unique video streams and not necessarily total duration. These users average about five TV programs per week versus three and a half movies.

While Netflix streaming was technologically limited only to PCs in its early days, the service was made available to Mac users in 2008.[37] The company has always been very clear about its strategy to be on every Internet connected device possible. And as of August of 2011, Netflix videos can be streamed on over 450 different devices. Three devices make up 45 percent of all Netflix streaming: the Sony PlayStation 3, Microsoft's Xbox, and the PC.[38]

Over the years, Netflix began to distance its brand identity as a DVD rental company in favor of an Internet video subscription service. In the second quarter of 2011, the company announced that 75 percent of new subscribers signed up for its streaming-only service.[39] With over 25 million subscribers in North America, some pointed out that its size—in terms of numbers of users—had reached that of cable giant Comcast.[40]

Hulu Plus Emerges As a Competitor to Netflix

On June 29, 2010, Hulu launched a preview of its premium subscription video service called Hulu Plus as a complement to its existing Hulu.com platform.[41] While Hulu Plus was also ad-supported, the biggest difference from "regular Hulu" is that it offers the complete current seasons of TV shows within its library as well as past seasons for select shows.

The service came out of beta in November of 2010 and was offered at a monthly subscription rate of $7.99. The company's goal was to reach one million subscribers by the end of 2011, which it exceeded ahead of schedule.[42]

In the second quarter of 2011, the company looked back on the growth of Hulu Plus since its launch eight months earlier. In addition to the fact that the number of full episodes had more than doubled, the amount of television series grew from 950 to over 2,100.[43] And like Netflix, Hulu Plus had made a big push to get itself onto connected devices, ranging from smartphones and tablets to DVRs and gaming consoles.

Yet Netflix remains the dominant force in terms of subscriber size at over 25 times that of Hulu Plus. And now that other players such as Amazon Prime and Vudu have entered the market, content availability and accessibility are becoming key differentiators.[44]

Television Gets Truly Portable Thanks to the iPad

The Apple iPad went on sale in the United States on April 3, 2010, and sold 300,000 units on its first day.[45] Nearly 15 million were sold within eight months of its first year, and 2011 estimates call for an additional 40 million units to be sold.[46] While deemed for a short while as the fastest selling consumer electronics device ever (only to be outdone by Xbox Kinect),[47] there is no doubt that the tablet device is having a major and permanent effect on the way people watch television.

Netflix was of course available for the iPad at its initial launch, as was ABC, who once again pioneered the notion of easy access to its full episodes. The iPad's ABC Player was heralded as one of the better designed apps during the device's early days; it gives users access to all of the same content that is available on ABC.com while taking advantage of the iPad's high-definition display.

The app's home screen is divided into two main areas. The top carousel rotates through seven different featured TV shows, displaying strikingly vivid episode artwork tiles. In the lower-third of each of the episode tiles, the program's name is displayed, along with the day and time it airs on broadcast. A large red "Watch the Latest Episode" button serves as a simple call to action.

The bottom of the screen defaults to the six most popular episodes across ABC programs between which users can alternatively toggle to view the latest episodes. Among the navigation commands at the very bottom of the application is a "Schedule" button that displays shows in a helpful program guide format. The "All Shows" option visually lays out each of the TV series available for streaming in alphabetical order. Selecting one prompts its latest episodes to pop up. ABC's data conveys that females comprise close to 60 percent of the ABC iPad Player's user base; the most popular streamed TV series is currently *Modern Family*. The app has over two million downloads and accounts for upwards of 10 percent of all ABC full episode online streaming.

Many other networks have since followed suit buy launching full episode streaming iPad apps. One of these was NBC, who updated its iPad app to include full episodes from 28,000 of its television series using an ad-supported delivery model similar to ABC's approach in September of 2011.[48]

HBO Makes Streaming Content Available Immediately After Its Broadcast

The HBO Go iPad app launched in early May of 2011 and had over 2.5 million downloads within six weeks.[49] But there was a bit of a twist to accessing its content; the cable network required users to authenticate themselves to prove that they are indeed HBO subscribers. Once they've done so, a user unlocks access to over 1,400 HBO shows, movies, and specials. The app, which is also available for the iPhone and Android devices, includes HBO original programming as well as behind the scenes extras. Customers are able to stream previous seasons of HBO TV series—including those that are no longer in production.

New episodes of HBO original series that are currently on-air become available to watch via HBO Go immediately after their first-run broadcast airing. After a given episode's closing credits, an art card appears onscreen displaying the following in bold block letters: "ALL CURRENT EPISODES OF THIS PROGRAM ARE NOW AVAILABLE ON HBO GO." This not only creates awareness of HBO's TV everywhere offering; it also helps underscore the recency of its content library.

When first launching the HBO Go app, new users are taken through a simple authentication process and asked to choose their television provider from a number of button-like options presented. After they select these, users need only enter their username and password for their TV provider account, and the app will keep the user authenticated for 14 days. One issue with this kind of authentication—which has become increasingly popular across TV everywhere—is that many people never or rarely use their pay TV broadband credentials, and must therefore undergo a somewhat cumbersome process to retrieve them.

The application's home screen automatically pans through video content art cards in an almost screensaver-like way. Each art card is clickable to its respective content. If a user wants to watch a specific TV series or movie, a navigation bar along the bottom of the application itemizes content by genre. Clicking the "Series" button lists all of the HBO originals through series screen art. Clicking *Entourage*, for example, will display all episodes for (current and final) season eight, and provide a drop-down menu to navigate to any of the past seven seasons of episodes as well.

The app also includes a number of extras, such as embedded Facebook "like" buttons and tweet prompts to encourage social media sharing. It integrates an HBO Go "Watchlist" that allows users to mark content they would like to save for later, or automatically add in new episodes to their queue as they become released for viewing.

There have been over four million downloads of the HBO Go app as of August 2011, and the company announced plans to distribute the application on game consoles as well as connected TVs.[50] This, after all, is "TV everywhere" in its truest sense: the ability to access consistent and reliable premium on demand content wherever and whenever one wants, regardless of the device they use to obtain it.

The iPad makes television viewing a truly portable yet still traditional "TV-like" experience. TV everywhere provides a great deal of incremental value to paying subscribers of HBO by providing countless ways for them to watch and experience the content they love—without charging them any additional cost. And the strategy may just be paying off; Time Warner reports that HBO Go users are watching more HBO programs than nonHBO go users.[51]

First on the iPad and *Then* on Broadcast TV?

While it has become commonplace for full episodes to be made available for online viewing *after* their broadcast airings, some television networks have experimented with the opposite.

On September 23, 2011, PBS released the first episode of its three-part Ken Burns documentary, *Prohibition*, to its iPad and iPhone streaming apps. This allowed audiences to experience the show 10 days before its official October 2 broadcast TV premiere.

As a bit of a bridge content adaptation, PBS's strategy was of course to generate buzz about the documentary by a set of connected "early adopters" in order to drive broadcast tune-in.[52]

Fox used a similar approach for its *New Girl* series premiere by making it available as a free iTunes download over 20 days before its broadcast debut on September 28, 2011.[53] While some were concerned that this move might affect the show's TV ratings, *New Girl*'s premiere episode garnered over 10 million viewers. As a result of equally impressive second episode ratings, Fox picked up *New Girl* for a full 24 episode season.[54]

The Xfinity TV iPad Application Blends Content and Utility

Though most major television networks now have their own versions of iOS and Android applications, they are not the only ones to offer TV everywhere solutions. In fact, pay TV providers like Verizon FiOS, DISH, and Comcast were some of the first groups to roll out streaming mobile apps.

The initial phase of Comcast's Xfinity TV app launched on November 10, 2010, and brought a new level of utility to the second screen.[55] Users are able to easily browse TV listings through an interactive television guide that leverages the iPad's unique features. Not only can users change their TV's channel from their iPad screen; they are also able to set and manage their DVR from any place that has an Internet connection.

Having this level and ease of remote access is perfect for those many serendipitous moments involving "watercooler" chatter about a TV show that frequently take place when people aren't physically near their cable box. People can use their iPad, iPhone, or Android device from anywhere in the world to instantly set up recording a TV show that they just heard about while it is still on their minds.

The Xfinity TV app also introduced a much more streamlined way to browse for video on demand content. Instead of the traditional VOD menu taking over the TV screen and exiting the program, the iPad application leverages the "second screen" to browse and choose content that piques interest. When ready, one needs only to click the "WATCH ON" button, which loads the requested content onto the big screen.

On February 1, 2011, Comcast rolled out the second phase of its TV everywhere app to include a highly anticipated "Play Now" feature. This tool gives users instant on demand streaming access to over 3,000 hours of television and movie content.[56] Users can filter the content by movies, TV series, or specific networks; or they can simply browse the entire library, which also includes HBO Go content for Xfinity TV subscribers who also have HBO as part of their premium cable package.

From On Demand to Live Streaming TV, the iPad Becomes a TV Set

At the Elevate Online Video Advertising Summit in June of 2011, industry executives estimated that 75 percent of television cable programming would be available on connected and mobile devices within two years.[57] And the portable content to which they're referring is not just limited to pre-recorded on demand video.

In a strange coincidence of art imitating life, a major news story broke on Twitter as I was writing this section. Without easy access to a television set, I immediately launched the CNN app on my iPad to verify the truth about the initial tweets, and was able to watch the story unfold streaming live on *The Situation Room* from my iPad as if I was in front of my TV.

I could do this because CNN updated its existing iPad application on July 18, 2011 to include a feature that streams its actual live television broadcast (including commercials) for both CNN and Headline News.[58] The application employs a similar authentication mechanism as HBO Go does for users who wish to "unlock" the CNN live stream. For those who cannot or wish not to authenticate, the CNN iPad app, by default, contains a lot of relevant and timely nontelevision content available outside of its "paywall."

CNN was certainly not the first TV network to offer its live television stream via the iPad. ESPN was out with the WatchESPN app across Apple iOS devices over three months prior to the CNN application upgrade. While similar in design, WatchESPN is limited to subscribers of only certain pay TV companies (Comcast is not one of them).[59] The app includes a helpful program guide that simplifies finding what is on and what is upcoming across ESPN, ESPN2, ESPN3, and ESPNU.

Cablevision managed to beat ESPN by just five days when it launched its contentious "Optimum" iPad application on April 2, 2011, giving its subscriber base access to over 300 live streaming television channels.[60] Some TV networks were not pleased with the move; media conglomerate Viacom even went so far as to take legal action (which was fortunately amicably resolved[61]). Time Warner Cable also caused a stir by launching the very first live television streaming iPad app with 32 channels on March 15, 2011.[62]

We would be remiss if we failed to acknowledge one of the original TV everywhere solutions: Slingbox debuted in June of 2005 and allowed users to watch their home televisions over the Web on a PC. Today's much smaller set-top Slingbox works with a companion SlingPlayer that is available on a number of mobile devices—including the iPad.[63] And on November 10, 2011, the company announced "SlingPlayer for Facebook," an app that allows Facebook users to watch and share TV directly from within the popular social network.[64]

Old Business Models Are Not in Synch with Today's Technology

The traditional TV set and the iPad have had an opposite evolution in regards to TV everywhere. Television, of course, started out with only live broadcasts, and eventually evolved to include video on demand. The iPad, on the other hand, launched with access to on demand episodes and is now starting to stream live television.

The technology to truly meet the promise of "anywhere/anytime" television content has been in place for some time now; however, the Viacom/Cablevision lawsuit is just one example that begins to highlight the fear that exists of cannibalizing tried and true revenue streams. Networks are becoming a lot more cautious; ABC's Vice President of Digital Media Rick Mandler puts it best:

> We've been very careful about what to do next; on one hand, we don't want to be in a position where we're actually providing the catalyst for cord cutting. On the other hand, we really want to keep moving forward. So we've come to a middle ground where we want to move forward with distribution partners. We want to get our stuff out there and be as forward looking as possible; but we also want to try to preserve the existing distribution system by requiring people to authenticate themselves as bona fide pay TV subscribers. It's a good middle ground: The consumer's going to get their TV anywhere; wherever they are, their TV is going to be with them. At some point they're going to have to recognize that they can't get something for nothing, and we can't be in a position where we completely disrupt the existing ecosystem.

Another network, Fox, made headlines on July 27, 2011 when it announced that it would only offer next day online streaming of full episodes to those who authenticated as pay TV subscribers. The rest of the public would now need to wait a full eight days from a given TV episode's first run broadcast until it was available to watch online.[65]

While this model theoretically seemed like the best possible compromise, its execution at rollout was lacking since only one pay TV provider (DISH Network) had partnered with Fox to be included in the authentication.[66] Pay TV subscribers from Comcast, for instance, were not able to authenticate—and were therefore techni-cally forced to wait eight days before they could access new Fox TV shows online. This caused video sharing sites to see large spikes in pirated Fox TV show downloads.[67]

When someone really wants to watch a piece of content at a given moment, they will find ways of accessing it. While we hope that they do so legally, many will rationalize the path of least resis-tance if it is easier to get that content in other—not always legal—ways. The onus, then, rests with the television networks and pay TV providers to smooth out any barriers to access content while still growing revenue.

The pullback of network TV content along with the need for greater monetization put Hulu out to bid for potential buyers dur-ing the summer of 2011.[68] On October 13, 2011, Hulu announced its decision to take itself off of the "for sale" market and instead focus on the company's strategic road map.[69] Hulu continues to show growth in ad revenue as well as paying Hulu Plus subscribers.

TV Everywhere or TV on Facebook?

On September 22, 2011, Facebook announced details of a major platform upgrade at its annual f8 developer conference in San Francisco. Among the many new features and changes were a number of deep media partner integrations. Facebook users can now watch TV shows from Hulu and Netflix without ever leav-ing Facebook. Using the Hulu "canvas app" as an example,[70] a person can watch videos that are instantly shared with their Facebook friends. That person can also see what their friends are watching and tune-in directly from the Facebook ticker or news-feed post.

The ability to comment allows for real-time discussions and fur-ther amplifies the content people are watching—therefore increas-ing the chance that others will discover it. This kind of "frictionless sharing," as Facebook refers to it, will not only increase the amount of data about Facebook's users but also make them much more micro-targetable to advertisers.

While Facebook is making it very easy to consume media within its platform, questions remain as to when, how, and to what extent audiences prefer to watch TV on Facebook (or other websites) versus the big screen.

Consumers Will Use the Best Screen Available

Content distribution deals are constantly being negotiated and renegotiated as the landscape unfolds. From a consumer's point of view, it is a bit like the Wild West when it comes to finding content. While the ability to watch "TV" whenever and wherever one desires has taken many steps forward, it is far from being an absolutely seamless experience today. Will Richmond, who is the editor and publisher of online publication that specializes in online video, *VideoNuze*, paints an accurate picture:

> If you think out to the nirvana end state, if there is such a thing, it would be a pretty cool world. You subscribe to pay TV, and all of a sudden, all of that programming that's available on your set-top is now also available on your connected device in another room in your house; it's available on your smartphone, and on your tablet. It's available whether you're in or outside the house. It's available on linear as well as on-demand. That's a pretty great future for consumers—but getting there is very complicated, and going to take a lot of work.

A few years ago, Nielsen stated that Americans will watch TV on the best screen available.[71] At the time, the living room television set was still their preference. But as technology and content accessibility continue to mature, so will consumer preferences for experiencing TV.

TV Everywhere Opens up New Opportunities for Advertisers ▬▬▬▬▬

Leverage the power of the platform. We get TV creative for digital platforms all the time. Each platform has unique capabilities and the creative should leverage the power of those capabilities.
—Rick Mandler, Vice President of Digital Media at ABC

While there are many similarities in features, functions, and user experience across various full episode applications, one fairly inconsistent element is each of these platform's respective advertising opportunities.

On one side, you have Netflix and HBO GO; neither of which have any advertising. On the other side of the spectrum are live streaming apps—including CNN, ESPN, and Cablevision—which directly mirror their TV broadcasts and hence, the TV commercials therein. Somewhere in the middle lies Hulu and Hulu Plus, the ABC Player, and other broadcast network full episode players. These tend to offer very customizable and platform-specific opportunities for advertising.

The ABC Player for the iPad serves in-stream ads at each regular commercial break in addition to a preroll before the episode starts. The number of ads served per break depends on advertising demand, which changes over the course of a year.

During the video ad's playback, a narrow banner along the bottom of the player counts down until the episode starts (or resumes) and includes a button in the lower right corner to "Visit Sponsor Website." Clicking the button expands the bottom banner into a frame that loads the respective website. A button in the upper left corner allows the viewer to return to watching the remaining video commercial.

Brands have the opportunity to submit advertising creative built-in HTML5 that opens up many new interactive possibilities versus a simple (and all too typical) video commercial. Instead, the ad could be a full-blown interactive experience, such as a game or tab-based user-interface. It could also include direct marketing acquisition from within the ad itself. The benefit in designing the creative for the tablet (or PC) medium is the ability it provides to contain the entire brand experience within the advertising unit itself. This increases the chances for a user to interact since they do not have to disengage from their intended content to a new window that loads a separate website.

Advertisers have the option to buy for just the ABC Player on the iPad. However, full episode media buys generally tend to include the player on ABC.com as well. This makes sense from an advertiser's perspective, since one is looking to align their brand to ABC programing wherever people are watching it.

Brands are not able to demo target their ads or insert them into a specific ABC show. Instead, they buy a bundle of impressions that are dynamically ad served across all shows over the course of their campaign flight. An advertiser will never know when or during what shows or episodes their ad will run. However, they can ask to be omitted from certain shows that may not align to their brand.

Hulu's Sweet Spot Is in Its Choice-Based Advertising Executions

Hulu offers a broad range of advertising formats at a load that is currently 25 percent that of normal television. There are, of course, the standard in-stream video ads that also include a clickable companion banner. For an added cost, the entire area around the Hulu video player can be branded while the video ad is playing to include a high-impact banner and color background.

Hulu's branded slate unit is an option for advertisers who want to make a first impression before a TV show begins to play. An art card with the sponsor's logo appears along with the copy, "THE

FOLLOWING PROGRAM IS BROUGHT TO YOU WITH LIMITED COMMERCIAL INTERRUPTION BY" and includes a voiceover that reads the copy and calls out the sponsoring brand.

One of Hulu's ad formats that has received the most attention is their "Ad Selector" unit. This provides viewers with a choice from either two or three options of what kind of video ad experience they would like to have. In its advertising spec sheet,[72] Hulu gives the example that "an automotive company could offer the user a selection of SUV, Truck, or Coupe advertisements. If the user selects 'SUV', the remaining breaks will playback commercials from the sponsor related to just to their area of interest (SUVs)."

The ad selector is a great example of a choice-based impression. Those users who actively make a choice at the selector screen (instead of simply ignoring it) end up getting ads that are more relevant to them. They will also be more receptive to viewing the ads, since they have been empowered with a certain level of control over them. As a result, studies have shown much higher click-through rates and ad-recall scores for these types of "choice-based" advertising executions versus regular video pre-roll ads.[73]

On October 3, 2011, Hulu announced its next evolution in choice-based advertising: giving its users the ability to swap ads with a completely different one. By clicking the "Ad Swap" icon when an ad begins to play, a user is presented with a choice of ads from various brands. These ads are displayed based on relevancy to the given user's Hulu profile. Not only is there no charge for those ad impressions that are swapped out; since the user has actually *chosen* the new ad, they're much more receptive to it. Hulu has conducted some early tests that show a 93 percent unaided brand recall on swapped ads with 35 percent of users reporting their intent to purchase the advertised product or service.[74]

TAKE ACTION: TV EVERYWHERE

As more and more consumers watch "television" whenever and wherever they want to, brands need to ensure they follow their target audience across devices. Here are a few pointers to help get you started.

1. *Design for the medium.* The notion and practice of TV everywhere has allowed people to watch a television show on any number of devices and applications. However, while the TV show transcends screens, your 30- or 60-second TV commercial does not. So be sure to design and optimize your creative around the behaviors of the channel and device on which it is running. Take advantage of the Web's interactivity.
2. *Follow the content.* It is hard to forget the episode of *Modern Family* featuring the iPad that Phil is hoping to get for his birthday. A surefire way to make your brand message portable across screens is to embed it into the content of the TV show itself. Integrating product placement as a nonblatant part of the storyline can generate a great deal of resonance. Look for branded entertainment partnerships with television series that are a natural fit for your brand.
3. *Give viewers a choice.* We have discussed at length that your message's impact is vastly more powerful when users choose to engage with your brand than when your ads are simply forced onto them. Whenever you can, leverage features like Hulu's ad selector/ad swap as a means to make your marketing dollars work most efficiently for your brand.

Television Programming Has Become Screen Agnostic

The days of watching TV only in the living room are but a distant memory. As much as television has always been a big part of our lives, its increasing portability is making it readily and instantly accessible to us at will. TV everywhere is yet another opportunity for your brand to be ubiquitous—everywhere your target is consuming relevant content.

Scan for More

Scan this QR code using your mobile device for videos and visuals of the examples and cases referenced throughout this chapter.

Don't have a smartphone with a QR reader app? No problem. You can access companion content directly by going to http://www .socialtvbook.net/tagged/chapter8.

Connected TVs

Blending Online Content with Television Content

Ezra Englebardt lives with his girlfriend Wendy in the West End of Boston, Massachusetts. Although he works as an Account Planner at a cutting edge digital marketing agency, Ezra—at age 31—considers himself to be an early adopter of technology gadgets.

While reading *Wired* magazine about seven years ago, Ezra was struck by an article that featured a device from a company named Roku that could be connected to one's television to display photos and play MPEG videos. He had already been hard-wiring his laptop computer directly to his television set to watch online videos since 2003, and used this same setup in 2005 when he started buying TV shows from iTunes.

Thinking about upgrading his jury-rigged Internet-to-TV set-up, Ezra tried out the original Apple TV device in 2007 but was underwhelmed with its performance. Then, in the fall of 2010, a handful of Internet-connected TV devices started gaining a lot more attention—perhaps due in part to Apple's complete redesign and relaunch of its Apple TV product.

One of the connected TV devices (as they became known) garnering its share of the spotlight was a familiar name to Ezra. Roku had just announced a new lineup of devices with its high-end model; at $99, it boasted full 1080p HD video streaming. A hint to his girlfriend's parents led to him unwrapping the top-of-the-line Roku XDIS beneath the Christmas tree in December of 2010.

Ezra and Wendy's Roku device is connected to their living room television, augmenting their existing premium cable package from Comcast. Sixty percent of their connected TV device's usage comes from watching movies and TV shows that the two of them enjoy together from Roku's Netflix app. Streaming television shows from monthly subscription service Hulu Plus makes up the next 30 percent. The final 10 percent of their Roku usage includes videos from Amazon Prime and a hodgepodge of other random content accessed through the player.

Their Roku device and Comcast cable box currently complement one another. Ezra and Wendy recently watched the first six seasons of hit Showtime program *Weeds* using Roku, and then caught up with the seventh season via their cable on demand library. Having easy access to shows like *Late Night with Jimmy Fallon and Modern Family* via Roku whenever they want to watch them alleviates Ezra's concern about remembering to set his DVR or have it reach its capacity of recordings.

The couple never asks each other, "Do you want to use Roku tonight?" It just sort of happens. Most of their television watching occurs on weeknights and weekends. Ezra and Wendy usually start by browsing the shows they have previously recorded on their DVR, which Ezra admits is constantly full. Roku is generally the second stop in their quest for television content and is always just one click away by using their remote control.

With the addition of Roku into their living room, "'There's nothing to watch' doesn't exist in our vocabulary anymore," says a confident Ezra—who was recently cleaning out his bedroom only to find two very dusty Netflix DVDs long-forgotten atop his bureau.

The Concept of Internet-Connected TVs Is Not a New One

On September 18, 1996—more than a decade and a half ago—WebTV launched to the public.[1] The brainchild of engineer Steve Perlman, who had worked at companies like Atari and Apple, WebTV's mission was to make the Internet accessible to regular households through their television sets. At that time, less than 15 percent of Americans had Internet access and the Web's capabilities were very limited in comparison to today.

WebTV's maiden product focused on basic online tasks such as Web surfing and getting e-mail. The device itself was a set-top box that was hooked up similarly to a VCR (remember those?) and additionally plugged into a phone line to connect to the unit's built-in dial-up modem. The box was heralded as the first stand-alone Internet-enabled device outside of a personal computer, thereby giving rise to the short-lived category name "Internet Appliances."

Sony and Philips Magnavox were the first two partners to manufacture and distribute WebTV, which initially cost about $400 if one were to also purchase its optional infrared keyboard. Retail sales over the 1996 holiday season were disappointing, and by April of 1997, WebTV had only about 56,000 subscribers. However, despite its slow start, Microsoft shared the company's vision and very much wanted to buy them.[2]

Steve Perlman and his WebTV cofounders struck a deal shortly after an Easter Sunday phone call from Bill Gates in 1997. At a conference in Las Vegas on April 6, Microsoft announced its acquisition of WebTV Networks for $425,000,000. With Steve Perlman serving as the president of Microsoft's WebTV division, the company focused its efforts on demonstrating the benefits of the Internet and positioning WebTV as a complement to television.

There were a few notable milestones for the product that would give a taste of what was to come many years later. Of the website referral traffic to E! Online, WebTV was its fourth largest source.[3] Microsoft also struck deals with a number of hospitality brands to make WebTV available in hotel rooms across the United States. In May of 1997, a partnership with Showtime enabled WebTV subscribers the ability to interactively vote on the outcome of the now-infamous "ear biting" Tyson versus Holyfield boxing match.[4]

WebTV Debuted Well before Its Time

In addition to the fact that 85 percent of Americans had never even been on the Web in 1996, the painfully slow download speeds of dial-up Internet connections made for a cumbersome experience when juxtaposed against the mature medium of television. WebTV tried to account for this by optimizing its Web page rendering speeds.

However, not only did WebTV have to teach people about the World Wide Web's behaviors; but because the device took over their television screens, it forced consumers to choose between watching TV *or* surfing the Web. WebTV was in no position to change a half-century's worth of television rituals. Add to that the extremely limited multimedia capabilities of the Web back then, which were absolutely no comparison to the crisp streams of broadcast television.

In 2001, WebTV was renamed to MSN TV, and the hardware has been discontinued, although Microsoft still supports its existing user base.[5] All is not lost, however. The concepts and technology behind WebTV went on to influence Microsoft's hugely successful Xbox product, which is the most penetrated "connected TV device" in America today.

A Lot Has Changed in 15 Years

Nearly 80 percent of Americans are online today.[6] Close to 180 million of them are watching about 70 hours of online video per month.[7] Over 70 million Americans now have high-speed broadband Internet access in their homes,[8] removing previous barriers to deliver rich multimedia-heavy online experiences to the masses.

Not only is streaming video usage on the rise, more and more people are tuning in to it during prime-time television hours. Historically, online video usage sharply dipped between the hours of 6 to 9 o'clock.[9]

With advances in technology and current human behavior finally in alignment, the fall of 2010 saw its share of connected TV-related announcements. On September 1, Apple revealed a completely revamped AppleTV device. On September 22 Roku launched its redesigned lineup of connected TV devices. Google TV-enabled devices hit Sony stores on October 6, and on November 10, the long awaited and highly anticipated connected TV, the Boxee Box, made its connected TV debut. Additionally, Forrester Research predicts that a third of US homes will have a connected TV device by 2015,[10] while eMarketer reports that 30 percent of US homes already have an Internet-ready television.[11]

Connected TVs Come in Many Shapes, Sizes, and Flavors

At their most basic level, connected TVs—sometimes called smart TVs or Internet TVs—all have at least one thing in common: they deliver online content that is directly displayed on the television screen. This, essentially, turns one's TV into a giant computer screen.

The appeal of connected TVs is that they provide the ability to watch online videos. A process traditionally relegated to a small computer screen is now available on a much larger display where people most enjoy a lean-back experience: the living room television.

Before connected TVs gained in popularity, there were some less elegant workarounds that involved wiring one's laptop into the television in order to display online video through the TV. This is what Ezra Englebardt did before he got his Roku connected TV device. However, one of the challenges in assembling it this way is that one may actually want to use their computer *while* they are watching their television—a preference that this setup rendered impossible. Therefore, the appeal of a connected TV is that it is persistently *connected* online; users do not have to constantly disconnect and reconnect the device.

Connected TVs also provide the added benefit of having a user-friendly graphical interface that makes it easy to browse and navigate to content sources. Since connected TVs are in effect computers, they each run an operating system and a wide variety of applications. Depending on the flavor of its OS, its applications may be referred to as widgets, channels, or simply "apps."

In fact, connected TVs are often evaluated competitively on the applications they offer. Most have weather and travel apps, and many even have social networking apps like Facebook and Twitter. Pandora and Spotify are popular Internet radio apps that have made their way on a number of connected TVs. But what most people *really* want is access to streaming video content. The make or break purchase decision often depends on whether a connected TV does or does not offer the Netflix and Hulu Plus apps.

Consumers want a simple way to easily access and stream premium movie and television content to their TVs, period. All of the other bells and whistles are simply value added features. Since connected TVs deliver content via the Internet versus cable or satellite, this kind of content is technically referred to as over-the-top (OTT).

The physical hardware that runs a given connected TV operating system can either be a separate set-top box device or an actual television set itself. While the user experience is virtually the same with either option, each comes with its own set of pros and cons.

Separate Device or Built-In?

Those who place their bets on a separate set-top box make the case that connected TV device hardware and technology is changing at speeds a lot faster than the six-year average replacement schedule of one's television.[12] Many of the set-top box device manufacturers refresh their product lineups yearly, and even more frequently in some cases. It is much more convenient and exponentially cheaper to buy a device to plug into one's TV than it is to replace the television altogether.

For those who opt instead to buy an actual Internet-ready connected TV set, Yahoo! has found that an average of close to 70 percent of its connected TV owners actually connect them to the Internet. However, that percentage varies by television manufacturer based on the ease of its initial setup. For instance, TVs that have built-in Wi-Fi tend to be connected at a much faster rate. And of the 70 percent who do end up connecting, 90 percent of them remain active monthly users of the TV's connected features. The key, then, is to find ways to entice and motivate people to connect their TVs when they first purchase them.

A "Connected TVs" study from Knowledge Networks published in June of 2011 revealed 22 percent of homes that have connected TVs but have not actually connected them to the Internet. Of that group, only one-fifth plans to connect their device within the year.[13] Their reasons for not connecting include their perception that they do not need the feature, or they prefer to stream content on the second screen (i.e., a computer or tablet device) versus the television set. Knowledge Networks estimates that connected TVs (that are actually connected) will be in 45 percent of US homes by the spring of 2012.

Since the promise and outlook of connected TVs is a very optimistic one, there are a number of key players in the space each trying to add their own competitive spin to the technology in order to differentiate themselves and gain market share.

The Second Generation Apple TV Boasts Way More to Watch

The original Apple TV began shipping on March 21, 2007.[14] However, it was not until the big reveal of its second generation model on September 1, 2010 that the masses began to take notice. At one-fourth of its predecessor's size, the new Apple TV raised the bar on design and setup simplicity.

Apple learned that its existing user base simply wanted access to HD movies and television shows, at lower prices, through a small device that did not produce heat or make noise.[15] A big part of the Apple TV experience is driven through iTunes, which continues to broaden itself from its music roots. As part of Apple TV's relaunch, the company announced the introduction of $.99 TV episode rentals—thereby increasing the ways in which Apple TV users could access television content to watch on the big screen. While the original device did not provide very much beyond its iTunes user experience, the new Apple TV launched with several other apps, including Netflix (which is a must-have core app on any connected TV device for many people).

Within seven months of its relaunch, Apple TV sold over two million units.[16] Then, in August of 2011, Apple TV released a software update that added a Vimeo video streaming app, as well as the ability to stream all iTunes purchased television content via Apple's iCloud product.[17] In late August of 2011, Apple eliminated the ability to rent TV episodes as it found its user base preferred to buy them instead and thus, interoperate with iCloud.

Roku Promises a Ton of Entertainment in Its Little Box

We're fighting against 60 years of embedded TV viewing behavior and it's really hard to change that. The only reason it's beginning to change now, in a meaningful way, is because it's a great experience that didn't oversell itself—but was available at a disruptive value proposition, which provides lots of stuff to watch for very little money.

—Chuck Seiber, Vice President of Marketing at Roku

Roku started out with a very simple mission: to get Netflix streaming on television. In fact, in 2008, Roku was formally part of the fast-growing movie rental company that later spun off into a separate entity. Netflix recognized that in order to be successful, they could not limit themselves to a single connected device; similarly, Roku recognized that its success as a streaming device could not be tied to a single source of content.

On September 22, 2010, Roku released an updated lineup of devices across three price point tiers. With its top two models supporting full 1080p high-definition streaming video, Roku was providing its growing user base with a reliable platform that delivered high-quality video at an affordable price.

Roku 2's July 2011 launch represented the company's first complete overhaul of the device's hardware infrastructure. Its newer, faster, smaller chip not only helped create a more compact physical design, but also enabled new features like casual gaming. Coupled with a Bluetooth motion-sensitive remote, Roku 2 became the first connected TV device to offer its users the insanely popular Angry Birds game.

The company began 2011 with one million customers and forecasted three million by the end of the year. Roku's user base is pretty evenly split between males and females. Although the purchasers of the device are 60 percent male, actual household usage is closer to parity.

With over 300 channels, Roku's biggest competitive advantage is its growing content partnerships and low price. The device is enjoying great success by focusing on doing one thing really well, versus trying to be the Swiss Army Knife of the connected TV space. As Chuck Seiber, the company's vice president of marketing, explains, "In this space, execution matters a lot and we think we've got a window where we can be established as a viable, alternative, reliable, and respected brand. We're always going to do something that's different and a little bit unexpected."

Google TV Will Get a Second Chance

The big force in the connected TV space, which is going to surprise many people, is Google—because they are basically replicating what they did in the handset space. They came out with a really bad first version of Android but then worked with all these different manufacturers who adopted the solution because the OS was free, open and offered a lot of different functionality to consumers. And I think the same thing is going to happen with their connected TV solution.

—Janko Roettgers, writer at GigaOM/NewTeeVee

After a lot of pre-release speculation and buzz, Google TV appeared in stores on October 6, 2010 in three different hardware formats. As a separate connected TV device, the Logitech Revue was designed specifically for Google TV. Sony's version, named "Sony Internet TV," doubled as a Blu-Ray DVD player and initially cost about a $100 more than the Revue. Sony additionally embedded Google TV directly into a line of television sets available in four sizes.

At its most basic level, Google TV acts as an interface layer that combines one's cable or satellite box content with Web content. A prominent search feature lets Google TV users simply type in a TV show name, genre, or other keyword; then the unified search results set appears onscreen and lists all options to watch, regardless of where the content originates. Some of the results may be TV episodes from online sources, while others may come from upcoming TV broadcasts.

Things got dicey for Google TV when, soon after its launch, television networks began blocking full episode video streams from their public websites to those watching them via Google TV.[18] While the TV shows would appear in Google TV search results, any attempt to play them was met with a rather cold message of device playback unavailability. This was by no means a technology issue, though; it was about money.

The irony, however, is that the full episode content in question was already publicly available on TV networks' websites. While it was okay for someone to connect their laptop directly to the TV in order to watch full episodes online through a regular Web browser, the ability to watch them through Google TV's Chrome Web browser created a bit of a firestorm. One after the other, television networks blocked video streaming access to Google TV users.[19]

Despite the ability to get content from lots of other sources on the Google TV platform, Sony and Logitech both reduced retail prices. Logitech launched a major advertising campaign that included TV spots featuring Kevin Bacon.[20] Still, Google TV went under the radar for awhile as they reviewed lessons learned and prepared for a relaunch of the product.[21]

Met with much optimism, Google TV gave a sneak peek of its redesigned interface at the Google I/O conference in May of 2011.[22]

A much more simplified user experience atop the latest Android operating system may just be the second chance that Google fans have been hoping for. The next version of Google TV will feature the Android Market, with new apps being added every day.

Boxee Says It Is the One Box Your TV Needs

> *There are a growing number of families looking to save money on their cable bill every month who understand Netflix and are willing to buy a device to get that on their living room TV. From this, they're discovering a whole other world of content that they can get on demand.*
> —Andrew Kippen, Vice President of Marketing at Boxee

Boxee first released a public beta version of its social media center software on January 9, 2010. The downloadable desktop application was based on its founders' vision that regardless of its format, video should be readily accessible and easily played on the big screen at the center of the living room.

On November 10, 2010, many Boxee users—who had been connecting their laptops directly to their televisions to watch video—rejoiced. The Boxee Box, a set-top device manufactured by D-Link, launched on Amazon amidst a great deal of anticipation. The box's sleek and tilted cube-like industrial design, illuminating a rescue green iconic logo, helps to bring Boxee's personality to life. A regular-sized remote with a full QWERTY keyboard on its backside makes for easy onscreen navigation and engagement.

Boxee's expansion from downloadable software to the connected TV device space was an important one for the company. Once the box is connected to the TV, it tends to stay connected and provides a much better user experience—for which Boxee is known. The somewhat hipster company is also known for nurturing a very vibrant, engaged, and loyal user community who, unlike Roku, are close to 90 percent male. (You can take a guess as to which one of this book's coauthors attended Boxee's RV backyard keg party at the 2011 SXSW interactive festival.)

After a major firmware upgrade in May of 2011 fixed a batch of initial launch bugs and gave Boxee's users access to Vudu and Netflix content, the Boxee Box was met with a stream of positive reviews.[23] As Boxee's own Andrew Kippen told us, "There are five apps that I think people look for when they shop for a connected device: Netflix, YouTube, Hulu, Pandora, and some sort of video on demand provider like Amazon or Vudu."

Boxee's embedded social media features provide its users with a constant flow of video recommendations from their friends, and enables them to share the content they watch and like on Boxee directly to Facebook and Twitter. The company launched its iPad app on August 8, 2011; it took many of Boxee's best features and optimized them into a truly social video experience designed for tablet interaction.[24] Boxee Box owners have the added benefit of sending video they are watching from the iPad to their TV screens.

As of August 2011, Boxee has close to two million registered users and has sold over 100,000 D-Link Boxee Boxes, which now have retail store distribution at Best Buy, Fry's, and Tiger Direct stores. In the fall of 2011, Boxee launched on its second device through a partnership with portable hard drive manufacturer Iomega. The company's growth strategy aims to get its software on many connected platforms.

Yahoo! Connected TV Was One of the First

Yahoo creates a personalized content experience that moves with the consumer to any device they are using including the TV, phone, tablet or PC.
—Russ Schafer, Senior Director of Product Marketing at Yahoo!

By the time you read this book, Yahoo! Connected TV should have made its way into an estimated 14 million households—at least, that is what the company forecasts.[25] Though the product first launched all the way back in 2009, many people did not know that Yahoo! was behind it, since their white label strategy significantly minimized any Yahoo! branding. The positive trade-off, however, is that Yahoo! Connected TV embedded its platform directly into 160 different TV set models across popular brands including Samsung, Sony, Toshiba, and VIZIO.

Like many new products, the first generation focuses on working out the kinks and laying a solid footing. A big part of that journey for Yahoo! was to emphasize the user experience, compelling content, and openness. Through Yahoo! Connected TV's free software development kit, developers brought many apps to life for the TV. Because they had high penetration yet low brand awareness, the product would take center stage in the fall of 2011, with major features set to launch incorporating the very latest in Web plus TV convergence. Yahoo!'s "broadcast interactivity" technology engages the consumer with Internet content related to what they are watching.

For example, if one happens to be watching a popular TV show through their Yahoo! Connected TV, the device audibly detects predetermined trigger points and prompts the consumer to engage in content related to that TV show. A subtle and thin black overlay with white letters appears toward the bottom of the TV screen, displaying a call to action to get related content or answer a poll question. Users simply click OK on their remote to open up a "sidebar" display that allows them to engage further.

As part of this launch, Yahoo! further released a set of second screen experiences enabled through a technology called "Device Communication." Yahoo! Connected TV viewers are able to use a smartphone or tablet device to receive and engage with companion content on the second screen instead of taking up precious TV screen space. (We detailed these kinds of "second screen" experiences in Chapter 4.)

A strategically notable addition to Yahoo!'s lineup of connected TV options—which traditionally had been televisions themselves—is a separate connected TV device manufactured by D-Link (who also makes the Boxee Box). The separate set-top box offers all of the features and functionality of Yahoo! Connected TV without having to buy a new television to run the platform.

Xbox Is a Lot More Than a Gaming Console

Chances are that the first word that comes to people's minds when referencing Xbox is "videogames." Yet the popular gaming console continues to evolve into a full-bodied connected media center that is now in over 53 million homes, where 40 percent of its usage is attributed to nongaming activities.[26]

The original Xbox was launched in November of 2001; its successor, the Xbox 360, made its debut four years later.[27] What gives the device its Internet connected soul is Xbox Live. First made available in the winter of 2002, Xbox Live now has over 30 million members who access apps like Facebook and Twitter as well as streaming video from content providers such as YouTube, ESPN, Hulu Plus, and Netflix.

Microsoft has recently seen its Xbox community stream over 30 hours of video per month per device; and time spent watching television content continues to make substantial gains. The addition of Xbox's popular Kinect product in November of 2010 made the process of interacting with TV content on the Xbox optionally controller-free. Using gestures and/or voice, Xbox Kinect users can easily browse Netflix and Hulu Plus libraries, and play and pause TV shows without even needing to pick up the remote.

Connected TVs Are Not Just About On Demand Content

There are four things we talk about missing out on through over-the-top platforms. The first is news, the second is sports, the third is what we call reality TV but includes things like American Idol,

and then the fourth is premium content like Entourage. For the first three, you'll start to see connected TV devices really make a push for some kind of integration with live TV.
　　　　—Andrew Kippen, Vice President of Marketing at Boxee

The next device on which Boxee runs will include an over-the-air antenna that allows its users to pick up HD programming broadcasting live via local TV stations. Roku has also been very clear on the fact that bringing live TV to connected devices is just a matter of time. The Roku device already offers a number of apps offering live feeds including Fox News, NHL, UFC, and Al Jazeera.[28] In September of 2011, Boxee announced a partnership with *Wall Street Journal* to bring its original live news programming to Boxee Box owners.[29]

In June of 2011, Microsoft announced that it would be bringing live television to the Xbox 360,[30] a move that would continue to shape the scope and landscape of connected TVs, how people use them, and their appeal to the masses. On October 5, 2011, Microsoft publicized a partnership with Verizon to bring a selection of live high-definition popular FiOS TV channels delivered via the Xbox and integrated with Kinect motion gestures.[31]

Verizon was just one of about 40 new Xbox media partners revealed by Microsoft. Others included Comcast's Xfinity TV on demand library, NBC Universal (which includes on demand programming from Bravo and SyFy), and HBO GO.[32]

Are Connected TVs a Threat to Traditional Pay TV Services?

Ilan Benatar is a documentary film editor living in Manhattan. After becoming frustrated with an $80 per month cable bill coupled with his existing disdain for advertising, Ilan began watching "TV" exclusively on his 27 inch iMac. He wanted an easy way to view videos on the TV screen without having to keep awkwardly connecting and disconnecting his computer. After reading an article on CNET a couple of years ago, Ilan became enamored with Boxee when it was just a desktop application, and was quick to order the Boxee Box connected TV device upon its launch. Ilan keeps his Boxee Box in sleep mode instead of fully powering the device off when he is not using it so that he gets near instant access to his content at a click of a button.

As a heavy user of Boxee's Netflix app, Ilan feels he has all of the content he needs when he sits down to watch television during the week. He is not an avid sports fan and he keeps up with current events using the ABC News app. He thinks it is "weird" that people still pay cable companies to watch TV, and claims that Boxee is saving him a couple of thousand dollars a year.

Ilan is a "Cord Cutter"—one of a hard-to-pin-down percent of TV viewers who have entirely given up their traditional cable or satellite services and found alternative methods to satisfy their television viewing needs. In many ways, the notion of "cutting the cord" is a bit of a statement that consumers are making: that they have had it with the high costs of pay TV.

The Amount of Cord Cutters Is .11, or 20 Percent, Depending on Whom You Ask

It doesn't matter that there isn't an exact percentage of cord cutters. What matters is why people are doing it and how this opens a window that allows us to see how people are going to use television in the future.
      —Janko Roettgers, Writer at GigaOM/NewTeeVee

It seems that a new statistic emerges every couple of weeks that attempts to quantify the severity of cord cutting. However, each source comes up with a very different number based on its relative point of view. In December of 2010, ESPN released a study that said only .11 percent of Americans have gotten rid of their paid TV subscription.[33]

Research firm SNL Kagan predicts that by 2015, 10 percent of US households will have cut the cord.[34] Roku reported that 20 percent of its customers are cord cutters[35] and a whopping 50 percent of Boxee users do not have cable.

To further confuse matters, a study by the Diffusion Group from July of 2011 cited the fact that 32 percent of Netflix subscribers are considering downgrading their cable subscription.[36] This, however, is not technically cord cutting, but instead referred to as "cord shaving."

In an attempt to thwart any material threat from cord cutters, television networks are beginning to pull in the reins to their online full episodes. As noted earlier, a number of networks have blocked access to their website's full episodes when they come from certain connected TV devices where an upfront agreement was not discussed.

In July of 2011, Fox announced that its TV episodes would no longer be publicly available the day after their broadcast, but would instead wait eight days before offering them.[37] However, those who authenticate as pay TV subscribers will have next-day viewing access. We address this emerging "proof of subscription" trend in Chapter 8.

Your Cable Box May Soon Become a Connected TV Device

There is irony present when we point to connected TV devices as a catalyst for cord cutting. The cable box itself is starting to look and behave just like one. As such, Comcast's Chairman and CEO Brian Roberts gave a presentation of the next generation of Xfinity TV in June of 2011.[38]

Brian's demo revealed a completely redesigned and interactive channel guide that includes recommendations based on what one is watching and/or DVRing. A suite of applications gives instant access to information such as weather and traffic, but also includes Pandora, Facebook, and Twitter. Xfinity's integration with Facebook uses one's friends' "likes" to help them discover new TV content.

What is missing from the Xfinity TV pilot at this stage is a Web browser and access to YouTube, Hulu Plus, and Netflix streaming apps. Without these services, there will continue to be a large gap between the cable box and the connected TV world.

The Opportunities to Advertise on Connected TVs Are Growing

Today, advertising within the connected TV world is still very nascent and falls within two main buckets: advertising on the platform itself, or doing so through the content apps that customers can access via the device.

The opportunities on the connected TV devices themselves vary widely. At one extreme there is Boxee, which has no platform-specific advertising opportunities as of yet. The company feels they are respecting the fact that their device is in people's living rooms and does not want to bombard their users with a lot of advertising.

Apple TV and Google TV are both also advertising-free, although it is very likely that the Google TV product will integrate some sort of advertising program as the platform stabilizes and matures.

Roku does have one display ad unit on its start page that, most of the time, advertises content that exists on the platform. Roku is open to the prospect of brands using that space; however, ad sales are currently not a big focus for the company. Their perspective on advertising is that it is far more effective when it becomes less like an ad, less invasive, and more complementary to the user experience.

Yahoo! Connected TV Has Robust Advertising Capabilities

A common theme that we heard from the connected TV players whom we interviewed was a prioritization of the product—both its user experience and content partnerships, first and foremost. Then, and only then, would there start to be a consideration for advertising opportunities. Yahoo!'s strategy took a similar approach by focusing on the user experience from its launch in 2009 until introducing advertising in 2011.

Yahoo! has leveraged its long history in online advertising to develop a well-thought-out platform for Connected TV, including support for display and video advertising. Launched with partner brands including Ford, Mattel, and Microsoft, Yahoo! Connected TV's advertising was designed to directly complement its user experience. By leveraging the platform's broadcast interactivity feature, advertisers can trigger a visual onscreen prompt that gives the consumer the option to view content related to the TV spot he or she is watching. The related Internet content can include product videos, voting, coupons, local deals, and even the opportunity to buy the product.

Similar functionality could also be used for a brand's sponsorship with a particular television airing. We give an example in Chapter 10 of Ford's sponsorship of the BET Award's social media lounge. If a viewer had been watching the event using their Yahoo! Connected TV, then a broadcast interactivity prompt could have *hypothetically* displayed and given those TV viewers the chance to engage more with the Ford Focus each time the BET awards cut to the Ford Focus Social Media Lounge on-air.

Xbox Kinect Brings Advertising Interactivity to a Whole New Level

In the spring of 2012, Microsoft will roll out "natural user interface ads" on its Xbox platform; dubbed NUads, these will incorporate Kinect's voice and gesture features.[39] TV spots being viewed on the Xbox can prompt viewers to take various engagement actions.

One scenario would include a prompt that instructs the viewer to audibly say "Xbox tweet." This would initiate an action within Xbox to share that particular ad experience with the viewer's Twitter followers. Another scenario will instruct the viewer to say "Xbox more" to get additional information about the product featured in the ad.

A third way to engage with an ad is to say "Xbox schedule," which would send the viewer a reminder about a scheduled event featured in the TV spot. Saying "Xbox near me" would pull up the nearest store locations for the brand featured in the commercial. And finally, a fifth scenario is a prompt to "wave," using gesture motion, if the viewer of the TV spot wants to participate in a poll relevant to its content.

While this is clearly some very cool technology, there are still questions yet to be answered as to the degree television viewers actually *want* this kind of lean-forward engagement with ads on their connected TVs.[40] However, the elegance with these kinds of advertisements is in their seamless integration with the unique features of the platform on which they are running. Both Yahoo! Connected TV and Xbox have designed advertising that caters to the behaviors and ways in which their users are already engaging with content.

Another Way to Advertise on Connected TVs Is through Apps

Many of the content apps that run on—and often across—connected TV platforms accept in-video advertising. For example, Crackle is a popular app on a number of connected TV platforms including Boxee, Roku, and Google TV. The app streams free, uncut movies and TV shows but is ad-supported with in-stream video. Since viewers are not yet able to skip these ads, there is a higher propensity for tune-in.

As connected TVs become increasingly mainstream, we will see new ad networks arise or existing ones, like YuMe, Rovi, and adRise, expand their scope to include bulk media buys within this space. Their appeal to advertisers may remain in their ability to buy more efficiently across devices and have access to a single dashboard for measurement and optimization.

Where Should You Start?

Connected TVs may seem a bit complicated and daunting for marketers at first. While still a relatively bourgeoning and niche market, your target audience is already engaging within it—albeit on a relatively small scale. Those platforms that are already offering advertising opportunities are pricing out their programs at pilot rates as this space continues to bud and eventually blossom. Given this, it is a fertile time to dip your toe into the connected TV waters.

TAKE ACTION: CONNECTED TVs

While we have already laid out a number of ways for your brand to take advantage of the connected TV space, the following are a few points we especially want to underscore:

1. *Match the message to the audience.* The user base of connected TV devices can vary widely. You must be careful, for example, not to run creative targeted at women on a primarily male-dominated platform. Approach this space with the mind-set that each connected TV solution is a unique opportunity and assess it accordingly.

2. *Emphasize the "connected" part.* Although the word "TV" appears in "connected TV," you are doing yourself and your audience a disservice if you simply run traditional TV commercials. Design your creative with engagement and interactivity in mind. This is the real power that comes from the convergence of television and the Web.

3. *Make it your own.* An app on a connected TV is a bit like a channel on traditional TV. If your brand has compelling content to share in a consistent serial format, consider creating your own channel that can appear (through partnership integrations) across a variety of connected TV devices.

The Connected TV Space Is Only Going to Grow

The Internet, indeed, has become television's best friend. Connected TVs represent a media channel mashup of epic proportions—one that brings audiences a whole new level of television content inter-activity and creates compelling ways for your brand to engage viewers. And this is just the beginning of a long and exciting period in the evolution of television.

Scan for More

Scan this QR code using your mobile device for videos and visuals of the examples and cases referenced throughout this chapter.

Don't have a smartphone with a QR reader app? No problem. You can access companion content directly by going to http://www .socialtvbook.net/tagged/chapter9.

Conclusion (for Now)

Connecting the Dots

At eight o'clock on June 26, 2011, it was show time for the eleventh annual *BET Awards*. Having set a goal of being the "most social" awards show ever, BET's strategy fired on just about every possible social TV thruster. And it all started well before the show went on-air.

BET looked no further than its very own *106 & Park* and leveraged the show's daily built-in, hyper-lean-forward viewing audience as a jumping off platform to promote the network's awards and drive tune-in. Two weeks prior to the awards show TV broadcast, the network announced "Fandemonium" on *106 & Park*, which tasked viewers with daily challenges to use various kinds of social media to express their loyalty to pop stars Chris Brown, Lady Gaga, Nicki Minaj, or Mindless Behavior. BET strategically chose to feature these four particular *BET Awards* artists due to their inherent and extremely active fans within the social web.

The brilliance behind the network's preshow promotional blitz was that they cleverly tapped into and energized the fanbases of BET's most socially engaged TV show *and* celebrity artists. Each Fandemonium challenge was designed at its core to generate volumes of valuable social impressions to amplify awareness of the *BET Awards*. For example, the first challenge asked *106 & Park* viewers to go to Facebook.com/TheBETAwards, "like" the page, and then find and "like" the photo of their favorite artist (out of the four) as a means of voting. Of course, each engagement action on Facebook resulted in impressions that promoted the *BET Awards*. Other Fandemonium challenges made use of Twitter, text messaging, and the *106 & Park* mobile app. The network also partnered with *BET Awards* show host Kevin Hart, who created a series of exclusive digital "bridge content" videos that were posted to BET's social media and other online properties as teasers in advance of the *BET Awards* broadcast.

During the actual show itself, BET employed a purposeful three-tiered Twitter strategy to help fortify and fuel the backchannel conversation. The network coordinated with seven celebrity artists, including Justin Bieber, who live tweeted during the on-air broadcast. A lower third overlay displayed tweets on-air not only from the celebrity artists, but also from the show's viewing audience. Additionally, as each award winner took the stage, a giant tweet wall featured fan praise as a dynamic backdrop to his or her acceptance remarks.

An additional partnership with TV check-in service GetGlue enabled the awards show's viewers to earn two possible exclusive stickers that each drove a number of social impressions. They could earn one sticker three days in advance of the show, signaling one's intent to watch, while the other was rewarded upon checking-in during the on-air broadcast.

BET.com created a second screen experience that featured live companion streaming video from six behind-the-scenes cameras, as well as the real-time Twitter backchannel. The official #BETawards hashtag, which flashed periodically on the primary screen, reminded viewers to participate in the backchannel conversations that were taking place on the second screen.

As a major sponsor of the *BET Awards*, automotive company Ford gave away a 2011 Ford Focus during the broadcast. Viewers were able to enter for their chance to win on BET.com prior to the televised event and then tune-in during the show for a secret hashtag to be revealed. Entrants needed to use this hashtag in order to complete their entry. The winner was announced live on-air in the "Ford Focus Social Media Lounge," which was hosted by TV personality La La Anthony, and featured a number of high-profile bloggers.

BET strategically decided to reveal the secret hashtag toward the beginning of the *BET Awards* show broadcast. As BET's Director of Social Media J. P. Lespinasse explained, "We knew that we wanted to push out that secret hashtag as early as possible. We shifted to La La in the social media lounge as we went to the first commercial break, and she divulged the secret hashtag. From a social media perspective, we wanted to generate big buzz early on in the show."

#BETFORDFOCUS became the number one trending topic on Twitter mere minutes after its on-air announcement. But it did not take a new car for the *BET Awards* to trend worldwide. In fact, there were over 95 separate trending topics related to the show that occurred over the course of the three and a half hour broadcast. In total, there were 7.5 million tweets about the *BET Awards* the day it aired, a third of which occurred within the Twitter backchannel during the broadcast itself. And from a social TV ratings perspective, Trendrr reported that BET was not only the top cable network in the month of June of 2011; the *BET Awards* was also the top cable *show*. The Nielsen ratings were equally as favorable, as the *BET Awards* ended up as the number one awards show in cable (at the time of its performance) in 2011, and the second highest rated telecast in BET history.[1]

The 2011 *BET Awards*' success stemmed from a solid foundation of great content integrated with a well-choreographed combination of social TV executions that managed to keep the actual broadcast as the key focal point. BET's Lespinasse said it best: "At no time did the programming people forget about the digital piece. The digital side also recognized that while we could have pushed for more tactics, we understood that this is a television show first and foremost. We ensured we weren't doing digital executions to the detriment of the beautiful production that went into creating this HD television program."

BET proactively looked to strike a balance between lean-forward and lean-back content elements to create a cohesive television experience that maintained its programmatic integrity, regardless of how deeply engaged each individual viewer chose to become. Yet with new apps, technologies, and tactics cropping up weekly (if not daily), the social TV space is becoming a bit crowded and fragmented.

Is Social TV Engaging or Exhausting?

I think that fragmentation among social media platforms is just going to grow. While the content seen across these different places is going to be consistent and will start on the TV screen, the audience will engage with the stories being told in many different ways. I don't see it ever merging into one clean user experience.
— Ryan Osborn, Director of Social Media at NBC News

Imagine the following possible, albeit exaggerated, scenario:

You turn on the TV and after flipping through the channels, you cannot seem to find anything to watch. You use your iPhone to browse what is trending on SocialGuide, and while scrolling through the socially sorted listings, you happen to receive an alert from BuddyTV reminding you that your favorite show is about to start. You reach for your iPad to launch the DirectTV app in order to change the channel on your DirectTV receiver. (You could have just used the remote, but you think it's more fun to do it from your iPad.)

The show you are currently watching is offering exclusive stickers from GetGlue, and you have four possible ways that you can check-in in order to earn them. Although you have the GetGlue app installed on your iPad and as part of the DirectTV onscreen experience, you reach for your iPhone instead and switch over from SocialGuide. After checking in on GetGlue, you take time to additionally check-in on both Miso and IntoNOW, since you have different people following you on each of the various check-in platforms and you want to let your social networks know what you are watching.

Since your television is powered by Yahoo! connected TV and the show you are watching is enabled with "broadcast interactivity," you are now seeing onscreen prompts with trivia and polls with which you decide to engage using your remote control. In addition, this particular TV series developed its own companion iPad app that you downloaded weeks ago. As you also follow along with companion content that's being delivered to your iPad, your iPhone is also receiving synched content that is being pushed out from Miso (due to its DirectTV partnership). Now you're receiving all kinds of enhanced content for your favorite TV series via your TV screen, iPad, and iPhone. You keep switching back and forth amongst the various screens, since the content that appears on each one is different—and you do not want to miss out on anything.

You are also following the Twitter backchannel conversation using the show's official hashtag. While the stream has been integrated into the companion iPad app—and is also available on SocialGuide—you are just using Twitter.com so that you can see trending topics and participate in different streams of backchannel conversations. Several celebrities are live tweeting, and some of their tweets are being displayed as lower-thirds on the TV broadcast.

You notice a TV spot during a commercial break with the Shazam bug displayed on it, so you launch the app on your iPhone and wait as it listens to and recognizes the ad to unlock special content. The next commercial happens to be partnered with Shopkick, so you switch to that app in order to earn an instant coupon. Meanwhile, the next TV spot serves up an onscreen poll through Yahoo! Connected TV that you use your remote control to answer. While this is happening, the advertiser used SecondScreen Networks to run a synched ad on the show's companion iPad app, which also happens to be a poll that appears at the exact moment the given brand's TV spot airs. You continue this cycle of lean-forward engagement throughout the one-hour show. So—how was it?

Although television is becoming a much more interactive experience, there is still plenty of opportunity for those individuals who just want to "veg out" in front of the TV. Extroverts who gain energy from socializing with lots of different kinds of people can have an engaging and energizing social TV interaction, while introverts who are looking for quiet downtime can still have a rich, more traditional, television experience. That is the beauty of the medium: social TV is choice-based.

Blurry Lines Add to the Complexity

What further complicates matters is that not only is the social TV space becoming crowded with new players, but existing ones continue to grow and expand their service offerings, which creates even more overlap. While it may seem from the way in which this book's chapters are organized that every company fits into neat boxes—well, that could not be further from the case.

SocialGuide is not only a social TV guide; it also offers social TV ratings. Yap.TV is a social guide that is also building out second screen experiences.[2] Trendrr is in the social TV ratings space but additionally conducts content curation. While Miso started out as a TV check-in service, it is quickly evolving into a second screen content delivery app. IntoNow is following suit with the release of its second screen iPad app.[3] Yahoo! Connected TV offers interactivity both onscreen and through its second screen companion iPad app. The Xfinity iPad app is a channel guide, remote control, DVR manager, *and* a TV everywhere platform. The Xbox originated as a gaming platform and has blossomed into a full-fledged connected TV. Conversely, Roku began as a connected TV device and is rapidly growing its casual gaming offering. And these are just a few of many different examples of the blurring lines of social TV.

The point of all this is that the current state of social TV is one of rapid evolution, revolution, fragmentation, and massive flux. Though the time will come when consolidation begins to occur, that is not going to happen any time soon. The industry is still trying to figure out what works based on consumer interactions and feedback.

At the end of the day, it is the television viewers themselves who have the power to determine which players continue to grow and which ones will ultimately exit the game. Their repeat usage of their favorite social TV apps and devices acts as a proxy for the ultimate "vote."

So What Is an Advertiser to Do?

In addition to the practical "how tos" we tried to convey within each chapter, we gleaned advice from many of the interviews we conducted as background for *Social TV*. We thought it would be helpful to hear directly from industry leaders the guidance they wanted to share with you:

> Brand advertisers face a big dilemma in the future of TV; although TV will only become more powerful in the future, the viewer's expectations of what the watching and advertising experience should be like are going to rise dramatically. And with many advertisers competing for bits and pieces of that viewer's attention, only a few are going to successfully use the right combination of platforms and interactive techniques to break through the clutter and create a memorable branding experience.
>
> —James McQuivey,
> VP and Principal Analyst at Forrester Research

> Social TV will enable Brands to provide viewers a "digital companion ad" on a second screen (laptop, tablet or mobile) that syncs to the exact second they view your branded message on the TV screen in the living room creating for the first time a fully integrated, geo-targeted and measurable direct response opportunity (think coupons, special offers, dealer locator, etc.) at the time the "emotion" of the brand message is delivered.
>
> —Andy Batkin,
> CEO at Social Summits, LLC

The activation is the piece upon which we need to focus together. What is the compelling call to action? Why, as a user, am I actually going to lean forward and engage? Sure, brands can embrace offers to do this; but rewards don't have to be tangible goods. If you tag a commercial and an MP3 shows up in your device, that's pretty cool. You just transcended two different screens and you brought me a very personal experience.

—Adam Cahan,
CEO at IntoNow

There will be a new advertising bucket in the future, which is the second screen—and companies will budget for it in the same way brands allocate digital, mobile, and TV. This new channel will be somewhat of a hybrid of everything in that it's TV plus digital plus mobile. We do know that people are using mobile devices while they're watching TV. So if an advertiser is spending a significant amount of money on TV, they should be allocating money in the second screen space as well.

—Somrat Niyogi,
Cofounder and CEO at Miso

Pay attention to all of the devices that people now use to watch TV. The second screen is becoming a really interesting place to bring branded content and ads that are relevant to what's airing on television directly to consumers and getting more direct feedback from them as a result which can help inform advertising media buys.

—Janko Roettgers,
Writer at GigaOM/NewTeeVee

Advertisers now have the ability to target more specific niche audiences than they ever did before. Because social media allows us to gather more direct feedback as to who's watching a show and what they think of it, advertisers can gain much better insight into who that audience actually *is*—versus the kind of information that you'd get from traditional measures.

—Christina Warren,
Entertainment Editor at Mashable

Brands should be thinking about how they can be a valuable part of the social conversation that takes place around a program. The social audience is there, and they want to be rewarded; they want offers and deals. This is going to start happening around linear TV.

—Sean Casey,
Founder and CEO at SocialGuide

The more open minded advertisers can be in thinking beyond just clicks or eyeballs with regards to how they're spending their money, the more they'll be able to be a part of this amazing evolution in how people are using social media and consuming television content.

—Jacob Shwirtz,
Director of Social Viewing at Viacom Media Networks

There's a lot of confusion in the space right now and a lot of different players and opportunities. My advice is just to *experiment*. If you're a brand looking to get on a connected TV platform, just make sure you build something that's cross-platform. Don't silo yourself into one platform.

—Andrew Kippen,
Vice President of Marketing at Boxee

Advertisers need to know their audience better than ever before in this fractured landscape. Having a Facebook page and a Twitter handle, creating rewards on whatever the check-in service may be; they all work toward different objectives. While it's an exciting time, you want to focus on what your own objectives are—but don't be afraid to experiment.

—Ryan Osborn,
Director of Social Media at NBC News

Think holistically. If you're a TV advertiser, TV is the centerpiece of your reach and marketing campaign. Then you have the spokes off that hub of the different digital platforms. If the campaign is holistic and integrated and works on all those platforms, it's got to be so much better than having a bunch of one-offs that don't talk to each other, that aren't consistent, that maybe have different brand messages.

—Rick Mandler,
Vice President of Digital Media at ABC

Advertisers have the potential to be the straw that stirs this drink. If they can drive the innovation, the programmers will get on board; there's no question. But I see the opposite occurring from my vantage point: programmers trying to get the advertisers on board.

—Andrew Wallenstein,
TV Editor at *Variety*

Advertisers should follow the creative lead of the best networks and shows—the ones that are engaging their audience—because you can take some of those examples and simplify them for advertising. A 30-second ad is a 30-second story. What lessons can we learn from the VMAs or *The Voice*, and how can you simplify that into capturing engagement within the ad itself? We should have the same bar for advertising as we have for shows. I can't wait until we get to work on a show where all of the creative we're putting into the show's engagement then flows into the 15, 30, or minute-long ads and creates its own little ecosystem of interaction. I think there's going to be a really great relationship there.

—Chloe Sladden,
Director of Content and Programming at Twitter

There were a few key and common themes that emerged across the many interviews we conducted, as you can see from the previous quotes: approach advertising from a cross-channel perspective, look for opportunities on the second screen, and most importantly, be open and willing to experiment and to innovate.

There are no concrete answers *yet* as to what works "best" in social TV. But that is no reason not to engage—especially in light of the fact that your target audience already *is*.

Television Will Only Continue to Change

On September 27, 2011, Sharp Electronics unveiled the world's largest LCD TV to date.[4] Measuring 80 diagonal inches, its television screen has more than double the overall picture size of a 55-inch flat panel TV. The AQUOS series television is also an Internet connected TV with built-in Wi-Fi, giving access to streaming video content libraries including Netflix and Vudu.[5]

Televisions will continue to get bigger, flatter, and lighter while simultaneously becoming smaller and more portable via mobile and tablet devices. They will gain higher definition resolutions and increasingly offer three-dimensional viewing. And they will get more connected, more interactive, and "smarter."

As the physical devices that deliver television programming to us continue to change, so will our behaviors in regards to those same devices. But the longevity of TV as a medium has less to do with technology and more to do with the actual *content*. Television is merely an empty chasm without the sights and sounds of its programs. As David Sarnoff wrote in 1939, "It is probable that television drama of high caliber and produced by first-rate artists, will materially raise the level of dramatic taste of the nation."[6]

Over 73 years later, content remains the greatest factor by which television success is evaluated and measured—and that is one thing that will *never* change. Geri Wang, president of sales and marketing at ABC, put it best: "I don't think anybody is saying '*I'm going to get this show picked up because there's a great social media app attached to it.*' It's the writing and storytelling first, second, and third."

What If *The Ed Sullivan Show* Was On-Air Today?

If the events of February 9, 1964 took place today, we might see Ed Sullivan himself live tweeting as The Beatles played onstage. The hashtags #beatlesmania, #FabFour, and #EdSullivan would most certainly be trending worldwide on Twitter.

A second screen companion iPad app would push out biographical content, polls, and trivia about Paul, Ringo, George, and John, and give television viewers many more details about John Lennon's marriage. In addition to exclusive streaming backstage content, users would also be able to instantly download "Till There Was You" plus the rest of the songs from The Beatles performance.

Those who checked-in with GetGlue would unlock a limited time "*The Ed Sullivan Show* meets The Beatles sticker," serving as a tangible piece of social currency that would forever remind them of this historical and resonant moment in time—one they got to experience because of the magical medium of social television.

Social media cannot save a bad TV show, product, or service. However, it can without a doubt enhance a good one. The opportunity is yours to reach and engage audiences by connecting television to the Web, social media, and mobile. The question is: will you choose to seize it?

Scan for More

Scan this QR code using your mobile device for videos and visuals of the examples and cases referenced throughout this chapter.

Don't have a smartphone with a QR reader app? No problem. You can access companion content directly by going to http://www .socialtvbook.net/tagged/chapter10.

11

To Be Continued . . .

Filling in the Gaps

Many people asked how we could write a book about a topic that was in such a massive state of flux. From the beginning the answer was an easy one for us. Just as television is converging with the Web, social media, and mobile, so too are books.

As such, we waited to write the last chapter of *Social TV* until just days before the book's publishing in order to bring you the very latest updates and happenings. To download Chapter 11, scan the QR code below using your mobile device or go to www.socialTV book.net/tagged/chapter11 from any Web browser.

This Is Not the Final Chapter

While Chapter 11 may be the last formal chapter in *Social TV* (the book), it is most certainly not the final chapter of social TV (the topic). We will continue to curate and post relevant and timely examples, cases, and stats on *Social TV*'s companion website at www.socialTVbook.net, where the exciting story of social TV and media channel convergence continues. . . .

Notes

Preface

1. http://www.bulova.com/en_us/legacy

Introduction

1. http://www.youtube.com/watch?v=U4hPX_PLC-o
2. http://www.bairdtelevision.com/RCA.html
3. http://books.google.com/books?id=r9sDAAAAMBAJ&pg=PA321
4. http://www.imdb.com/title/tt0043208/episodes#year-1952
5. http://www.youtube.com/watch?v=yQJjbJQdymA&feature=related
6. http://www.imdb.com/title/tt0075572/
7. http://www.youtube.com/watch?v=XSvGdfOfLFw
8. http://www.imdb.com/title/tt0697814/
9. http://www.imdb.com/title/tt0319931/episodes#season-1
10. http://www.youtube.com/watch?v=xffOCZYX6F8
11. http://www.youtube.com/watch?v=R55e-uHQna0
12. http://www.nielsen.com/us/en/insights/reports-downloads/2011/cross
    -platform-is-the-new-norm.html

Chapter 1   The Backchannel

1. http://www.edsullivan.com/artists/the-beatles/
2. http://www.imdb.com/title/tt0040053/
3. http://www.youtube.com/watch?v=vBGtsKyVYE0&feature=related
4. http://www.youtube.com/watch?v=Q1wIXIFfrXI
5. http://www.nytimes.com/2009/02/28/business/media/28network
    .html?pagewanted=2&hp
6. http://blog.nielsen.com/nielsenwire/online_mobile/video-jon-gibs
    -talks-about-tv-getting-social/

7. http://www.forrester.com/rb/Research/updated_2011_use_social_media_to_boost/q/id/60495/t/2

8. http://www.fastcompany.com/magazine/151/twitter-by-the-numbers.html

9. http://blog.twitter.com/2011/06/200-million-tweets-per-day.html

10. http://blog.twitter.com/2011/09/one-hundred-million-voices.html

11. http://www.wired.com/playbook/2011/07/world-cup-tweet-record/

12. http://thenextweb.com/twitter/2011/08/29/beyonces-baby-bump-reveal-at-the-mtv-vmas-sparks-record-8868-tweets-per-second/

13. http://www.facebook.com/press/info.php?statistics

14. http://www.timewarner.com/newsroom/press-releases/2009/01/CNN_Digital_No1_on_Inauguration_Day_Sets_Record_for_01-23-2009.php

15. http://www.marketingcharts.com/direct/tweeters-more-engaged-with-tv-shows-18253/

16. http://allthingsd.com/20100608/why-tv-still-wont-embrace-the-web-quite-yet/

17. http://www.tvguide.com/News/Most-Social-NCIS-Idol-1033024.aspx

18. http://www.lostremote.com/2011/02/13/hey-grammys-you-cant-tape-delay-social-media/

19. http://www.nytimes.com/2011/04/23/arts/television/doctor-who-us-premiere-will-not-be-delayed.html?_r=1

20. http://www.mtv.com/news/articles/1621715/twitter-traffic-triples-during-video-music-awards.jhtml

21. http://tvbythenumbers.zap2it.com/2009/09/16/mtv-com-web-traffic-spikes-after-kanye-west-taylor-swift-vma-episode/27412/

22. http://media.twitter.com/twitter-tv

23 http://mashable.com/2011/09/12/cbs-fall-tv-social-media/

24. http://www.lostremote.com/2011/11/04/cbs-cranks-upsocial-media-for-november-sweeps/

25. http://mashable.com/2011/06/15/the-voice-social-medianbc/

26. http://adage.com/article/the-media-guy/inside-social-media-triumph-nbc-s-voice/228534/

27. http://mashable.com/2011/02/02/audi-super-bowl-twitter-hashtag/

28. http://www.reuters.com/article/2011/03/07/audi-idUSFAB01595620110307

29. http://www.mikeproulx.com/harmonicaftershock/2011/04/social2011-social-tv-presentation-extras.html

Chapter 2   Social TV Guides

1. http://www.tvhistory.tv/tv_forecast.htm
2. http://www.newsfromme.com/archives/2005_10_08.html
3. http://www.amazon.com/TV-Guide-Official-Collectors-Celebrating/dp/0977292711
4. http://www.bukisa.com/articles/233107_ten-most-valuable-tv-guide-covers
5. http://www.cartoonbrew.com/old-brew/rip-tv-guide-1952-2005.html
6. http://www.blurbwire.com/topics/Electronic_program_guide::sub::History
7. http://www.prevueguide.com/index.php/Prevue_Channel
8. http://www.tribunemediaservices.com/products-and-services/television/data/
9. http://www.itvdictionary.com/epg_ipg.html
10. http://expway.com/telechargement/1220546068.pdf
11. http://gigaom.com/video/yap-tv-v3/
12. http://www.lostremote.com/2011/08/10/yap-tv-debuts-eye-catching-social-tv-update/
13. http://mashable.com/2011/08/11/yap-tv-3-0/
14. http://techcrunch.com/2011/07/26/buddytv-iphone/
15. http://www.buddytv.com/buddytv-guide.aspx
16. http://www.readwriteweb.com/archives/facebook_read_watch_listen_3_major_implications.php

Chapter 3   TV Check-In Services

1. http://mashable.com/2009/10/26/getglue-2/
2. http://semanticweb.com/glue-gets-game_b469
3. http://mashable.com/2010/09/10/getglue-ipad/
4. http://getglue.com/stickers/groups
5. http://blog.getglue.com/?p=9330
6. http://blog.getglue.com/?p=8976
7. http://www.lostremote.com/2011/06/27/getglue-sets-tv-show-premiere-record/
8. http://blog.getglue.com/?p=7934
9. http://www.readwriteweb.com/archives/miso_a_foursquare-like_app_for_homebodies.php

10. http://somrat.tumblr.com/post/372994174/what-i-learned-about-the
    -douchebag-badge

11. http://gigaom.com/video/miso-competitive-reality/

12. http://www.lostremote.com/2011/05/19/miso-branches-out-with
    -social-tv-app-gallery/

13. http://mashable.com/2011/02/18/shaq-philo/

14. http://socialtimes.com/shaq_b39207

15. http://gigaom.com/2011/08/04/localresponse-acquires-philo-to-target
    -tv-check-ins/

16. http://reviews.cnet.com/8301-19512_7-20029921-233.html

17. http://mashable.com/2011/04/06/intonow-discussions/

18. http://mashable.com/2011/01/31/intonow/

19. http://gigaom.com/video/yahoo-intonow/

20. http://thenextweb.com/insider/2011/04/25/how-intonow-just
    -screwed-itself-out-of-millions-by-selling-to-yahoo/

21. http://www.lostremote.com/2011/07/28/intonow-partners-with
    -project-runway-launches-on-android/

22. http://www.marketingcharts.com/direct/tweeters-more-engaged-with
    -tv-shows-18253/tvguide-why-share-july-2011jpg/

23. http://blog.getglue.com/?p=7736

24. http://blog.gomiso.com/2011/03/15/most-miso-users-check-in-when
    -shows-start/

25. http://www.hhcc.com/blog/2011/07/get-ready-to-see-more-%E2%
    80%9Ctag-bugs%E2%80%9D-on-tv-spots/

26. http://www.shazam.com/music/web/pressrelease.html?nid=NEWS
    20080710151044

27. http://www.shazam.com/music/web/pressrelease.html?nid=NEWS
    20100120083433

28. http://www.shazam.com/music/web/pressrelease.html?nid=NEWS
    20110217092300

29. http://www.shazam.com/music/web/pressrelease.html?nid=NEWS
    20110120092223

30. http://paidcontent.org/article/419-shazam-takes-another-32-million
    -funding/

31. http://mashable.com/2010/08/16/best-buy-shopkick-rewards/

32. http://www.fastcompany.com/1765619/how-shopkick-became-more
    -charitable-by-going-for-profit

33. http://mashable.com/2011/02/14/shopkick-checkins/
34. http://www.nytimes.com/2011/05/19/business/media/19adco.html
35. http://blog.getglue.com/?p=6124
36. http://blog.getglue.com/?p=8266
37. http://blog.getglue.com/?p=9143
38. http://www.videonuze.com/blogs/?2011-08-03/TV-Guide-Updates
    -Watchlist-App-With-Social-Features-and-New-Video-Sources/&id=3165

Chapter 4   The Second Screen

1. http://blog.nielsen.com/nielsenwire/online_mobile/three-screen
   -report-q409/
2. http://www.yume.com/content/ipg-media-lab
3. http://www.tvweek.com/news/2011/05/when_it_comes_to_ad_avoid
   ance.php
4. http://www.lostremote.com/2011/07/05/prime-time-for-mobile-devices
   -same-as-tv/
5. http://www.futureofmediaevents.com/2011/01/26/study-86-of-people
   -use-mobile-devices-while-watching-tv/
6. http://gigaom.com/2011/05/18/tablet-penetration-only-5-percent-but
   -growth-is-promising/
7. http://www.lostremote.com/2011/05/20/ipad-users-spend-most-time
   -in-front-of-tv/
8. http://blog.nielsen.com/nielsenwire/online_mobile/in-the-u-s-tablets
   -are-tv-buddies-while-ereaders-make-great-bedfellows/
9. http://blog.nielsen.com/nielsenwire/online_mobile/nielsen-and-abcs
   -innovative-ipad-app-connects-new-generation-of-viewers/
10. http://www.mikeproulx.com/harmonicaftershock/2010/09/web-tv
    -convergence-abcs-my-generation-ipad-app.htmlX
11. http://www.cnn.com/2011/TECH/mobile/01/31/greys.anatomy.interac
    tive/index.html
12. http://www.lostremote.com/2011/02/11/fox-debuts-ipad-app-that
    -syncs-with-tv-show-bones/
13. http://tvbythenumbers.zap2it.com/2011/02/09/ipad-envy-alert-ulti
    mate-must-have-companion-bones-ipad-app-launches-today/
14. http://paidcontent.org/article/419-exclusive-weather-channel-syncs
    -up-with-ipad/

15. http://www.weather.com/tv/tvshows/peterlik/article/About_The_Show
    _2011-01-18
16. http://mlb.mlb.com/mobile/atbat/
17. http://www.lostremote.com/2011/04/24/nba-ipad-app-offers-real-time
    -experience-during-playoffs/
18. http://www.youtube.com/watch?v=9bANdNzsuFo
19. http://www.imdb.com/title/tt1718045/
20. http://www.mikeproulx.com/harmonicaftershock/2011/04/the-social
    -ratings-of-the-kennedys-reelzchannel.html
21. http://www.youtube.com/watch?v=2hgvu3RVw6A
22. http://www.lostremote.com/2011/05/03/how-people-watched-the
    -royal-wedding-on-nbc/
23. http://paidcontent.org/article/419-bravo-now-ipad-app-launched-to
    -promote-season-finale-of-bethenny/
24. http://blogs.discovery.com/discovery-insider/2011/03/discovery-chan
    nel-app-for-ipad-launch.html
25. http://www.lostremote.com/2011/08/01/new-discovery-apps-take
    -shark-week-fans-up-close/
26. http://www.insidefacebook.com/2011/05/23/usa-network-chatter-tv/
27. http://blog.gomiso.com/2011/09/01/miso-connects-social-tv-to-directv/
28. http://gomiso.com/dexter
29. http://dl.dropbox.com/u/2849649/The_Miso_Sync_Experiment.pdf
30. http://weblogs.variety.com/on_the_air/2011/11/xtra-factor-app-off-to
    -solid-start.html
31. http://www.secondscreen.com/how-it-works
32. http://www.heinekeninternational.com/270411_heineken_launches
    _dualscreen_game.asp
33. http://www.appmarket.tv/news/1242-akqa-wins-cannes-lions-gold
    -for-heinekens-starplayer-a-dual-screen-football-gaming-app-with
    -real-time-engagement.html

Chapter 5   Social TV Ratings

1. http://abcmedianet.com/web/dnr/dispDNR.aspx?id=100207_05
2. http://www.npr.org/blogs/monkeysee/2009/04/jumping_on_the
    _chuck_wagon_nbc.html
3. http://www.airlockalpha.com/node/8750/chuck-still-struggling-to
    -keep-audience.html

4. http://www.aoltv.com/2009/04/28/hmmm-nbc-com-is-calling-the
-chuck-season-finale-a-series-fi/
5. http://www.givememyremote.com/remote/2009/04/06/be-a-nerdjoin
-the-herd-save-chuck/
6. http://mashable.com/2009/04/27/nbc-chuck/
7. http://adage.com/article/madisonvine-news/subway-caught-fan-effort
-save-nbc-tv-series-chuck/136301/
8. http://www.youtube.com/watch?v=uDtePZ1MFT0
9. http://www.nbc.com/news/2009/05/19/nbc-renews-popular-action-com
edy-chuck-for-the-2009-2010-season-with-subway-as-major-sponsor/
10 http://www.communicationencyclopedia.com/public/tocnode?id=
g9781405131995_yr2011_chunk_g978140513199519_ss41-1
11. http://www.washingtonpost.com/wp-srv/style/tv/permanent/faqniel
sen.htm
12. http://www.rbr.com/tv-cable/nielsen-re-ranks-the-dmas-for-the-new
-tv-season.html
13. http://www.hhcc.com/blog/2010/10/nielsen-tv-ratings-meet-twitter
-sentiment/
14. http://blog.nielsen.com/nielsenwire/online_mobile/the-relationship
-between-social-media-buzz-and-tv-ratings/
15. http://www.lostremote.com/2011/09/08/trendrr-reveals-most-antici
pated-fall-tv-pilots/
16. http://gigaom.com/video/twitter-weather-channel-social-integration/
17. http://blog.trendrr.com/2011/08/10/the-weather-channel-technical
-challenges-and-solutions/
18. http://socialguide.com/social100
19. http://adage.com/article/trending-topics/sad-ballad-sinking-social
-engagement-glee/230094/

Chapter 6   Bridge Content

1. http://www.imdb.com/title/tt0077000/episodes
2. http://jabartlett.wordpress.com/2011/03/21/one-day-in-your-life
-march-21-1980/
3. http://www.youtube.com/watch?v=cfqNjlfAn6EX
4. http://abcnews.go.com/Entertainment/story?id=115018&page=1
5. http://www.people.com/people/archive/article/0,,20076970,00.html
6. http://www.time.com/time/magazine/article/0,9171,924376-9,00.html

7. http://uselectionatlas.org/RESULTS/national.php?year=1980
8. http://www.nfl.com/superbowl/story/09000d5d8164bc7b/article/ super-bowl-xliv-beats-mash-finale-for-us-viewership-record
9. http://www.people.com/people/archive/article/0,,20077838,00.html
10. http://www.marketingcharts.com/direct/tweeters-more-engaged-with -tv-shows-18253/tvguide-when-talk-july-2011jpg/
11. http://www.insidefacebook.com/2011/05/18/tv-shows-facebook -television/
12. http://www.lostremote.com/top-tv-social-media/
13. http://www.business2community.com/social-media/10-ways-to -extend-your-brand's-reach-on-facebook-014765
14. http://www.allfacebook.com/shocker-3-to-7-5-of-fans-see-your-pages -posts-2011-06
15. http://www.facebook.com/press/info.php?statistics
16. http://www.bloomberg.com/news/2011-05-25/music-tv-are-next -social-frontiers-zuckerberg.html
17. http://www.mikeproulx.com/harmonicaftershock/2008/05/how-i-met -your.html
18. http://www.imdb.com/title/tt0090417/
19. http://www.imdb.com/title/tt0791930/
20. http://www.teennick.com/shows/degrassi/episode-guide
21. http://www.ovguide.com/battlestar-galactica-(the-miniseries)-9202a8c 04000641f80000000009aaffd
22. http://www.imdb.com/title/tt0407362/episodes
23. http://www.nytimes.com/2006/09/05/arts/television/05gala.html
24. http://www.imdb.com/title/tt0765425/episodes
25. http://schedule.sxsw.com/events/event_IAP6348
26. http://www.buddytv.com/articles/greys-anatomy/sesame-street-tv-par odies-old-38341.aspx
27. http://www.youtube.com/watch?v=5SvHYkAKU88

Chapter 7   Audience Addressability

1. http://www.tvhistory.tv/tv_forecast.htm
2. http://www.tvacres.com/broad_commercials.htm
3. http://www.adweek.com/news/television/4as-whats-delaying-ad -addressability-101758
4. http://visibleworld.com/Connect/Solutions/Resources

5. http://invidi.com/itc_company.html
6. http://www.adweek.com/news/television/smg-comcast-addressable
-system-cuts-ad-skipping-101636
7. http://www.canoe-ventures.com/about.php

Chapter 8 TV Everywhere

1. http://www.visions4.net/journal/time-line/
2. http://www.japaninc.net/top-10-japanese-inventions/
3. http://books.google.com/books?id=75dRYTqixzYC&lpg=PA116&dq=s
ony%20watchman%20and%20popular%20science&pg=PA116#v=one
page&q&f=false
4. http://books.google.com/books?id=xEBz2cN3sw8C&lpg=PA34
-IA3&dq=sony%20watchman&pg=PA34-IA3#v=onepage&q=
sony%20watchman&f=false
5. http://www.youtube.com/watch?v=iIIc-VEuGec
6. http://www.time.com/time/specials/packages/article/0,28804,2023
689_2023681_2023599,00.html
7. http://gigaom.com/video/video-a-few-last-moments-with-the-sony
-watchman/
8. http://www.medialit.org/reading-room/video-here-stay
9. http://www.tivo.com/jobs/questions/history-of-tivo/index.html
10. http://news.cnet.com/New-TV-recording-devices-due-soon/2100
-1040_3-223631.html
11. http://www.nytimes.com/1999/10/02/business/tivo-rises-24-in-its-sec
ond-day.html
12. http://tvbythenumbers.zap2it.com/2011/03/23/dvr-penetration-grows
-to-39-7-of-households-42-2-of-viewers/86819/
13. http://gigaom.com/video/dvr-usage-nielsen/
14. http://blog.nielsen.com/nielsenwire/media_entertainment/do-ameri
cans-watch-more-dvrd-commercials-than-you-think/
15. http://news.cnet.com/Video-on-demand-may-trouble-digital-video
-recording-upstarts/2100-1040_3-234765.html
16. http://www.forbes.com/2000/07/29/feat4.html
17. http://www.businessweek.com/archives/2000/b3694163.arc.htm
18. http://www.engadget.com/2011/04/27/comcast-is-first-with-vod-from
-all-four-major-networks-still-ne/

19. http://blog.comcast.com/2011/05/xfinity-on-demand-reaches-20-billion-views.html

20. http://www.lostremote.com/2011/05/27/the-most-watched-tv-shows-on-comcast-xfinity/

21. http://blogs.adobe.com/dreaming/2006/05/abc_launces_full_episode_strea.html

22. http://www.laughingplace.com/News-ID10025400.asp

23. http://mediadecoder.blogs.nytimes.com/2007/12/05/viewers-turning-to-the-web-for-tv/

24. http://www.harrisinteractive.com/NewsRoom/HarrisPolls/tabid/447/mid/1508/articleId/817/ctl/ReadCustom%20Default/Default.aspx

25. http://www.hulu.com/press/new_video_venture.html

26. http://newteevee.com/2008/08/19/hulu-hit-105m-streams-in-july/

27. http://mashable.com/2010/11/10/hulu-stats/

28. http://blog.hulu.com/2011/02/02/stewart-colbert-and-hulus-thoughts-about-the-future-of-tv/

29. http://gigaom.com/video/more-video-ads/

30. http://www.nytimes.com/2010/11/23/business/media/23adco.html?_r=1&ref=business

31. http://team3netflix.blogspot.com/

32. http://www.businessweek.com/investor/content/jan2007/pi20070116_700685.htm

33. http://paidcontent.org/article/419-digitalhome-netflix-balances-the-benefits-and-costs-of-broadband/

34. http://mashable.com/2010/12/02/netflix-newer-tv-content/

35. http://thenextweb.com/media/2011/02/22/netflix-signs-streaming-deal-with-cbs-now-carries-all-4-major-us-networks/

36. http://www.knowledgenetworks.com/news/releases/2011/090811_ott-video.html

37. http://blog.netflix.com/2007/08/instant-watching-on-mac-firefox-and.html

38. http://gigaom.com/video/netflix-by-the-numbers/

39. http://www.digitaltrends.com/home-theater/75-percent-of-new-netflix-subscriptions-in-q2-were-streaming-only/

40. http://techcrunch.com/2011/04/25/netflix-now-as-big-as-comcast-cable/

41. http://blog.hulu.com/2010/06/29/introducing-hulu-plus-more-wherever-more-whenever-than-ever

42. http://paidcontent.org/article/419-kilar-hulu-plus-subs-will-pass-1 -million-ahead-of-schedule/
43. http://blog.hulu.com/2011/07/06/q2/
44. http://paidcontent.org/article/419-how-netflix-hulu-and-amazon -stack-up/
45. http://betanews.com/2010/04/05/apple-announces-first-day-ipad-sales/
46. http://www.appleinsider.com/articles/11/07/27/ubs_ups_2011_ipad _estimate_to_39_9m_63_market_share.html
47. http://www.pcworld.com/article/221738/kinect_breaks_guinness _record_sells_10_million_systems_tops_iphone_and_ipad.html
48. http://www.digitaltrends.com/apple/tnt-nbc-and-tbs-bring-full-length -tv-episodes-to-ipad-for-free/
49. http://www.videonuze.com/blogs/?2011-06-15%2018:25:47/-Cable -Show-HBO-GO-Has-2-6-Million-Downloads-Watch-ESPN-Has-2 -Million-Downloads/&id=3103
50. http://www.digitaltrends.com/gaming/hbo-go-is-coming-to-game -consoles-and-connected-tvs/
51. http://www.pbs.org/mediashift/2011/08/hbo-go-app-shakes-up-the -streaming-tv-scene229.html
52. http://gigaom.com/apple/new-ken-burns-documentary-to-debut-on -ipad-and-iphone/
53. http://allthingsd.com/20110906/now-on-itunes-for-free-a-show-you -cant-watch-on-fox-for-a-couple-weeks/
54. http://gigaom.com/video/new-girl-online-success/
55. http://www.hhcc.com/blog/2010/11/3-screen-convergence-the-xfinity -ipad-app/
56. http://paidcontent.org/article/419-first-look-comcast-xfinity-flips-the -switch-on-ipad-streaming/
57. http://www.videonuze.com/blogs/?2011-06-10%2010:06:04/-ELEVATE -75-of-Cable-TV-Programming-to-be-on-TV-Everywhere-in-2-Years/ &id=3098
58. http://techcrunch.com/2011/07/18/cnn-tv-everywhere/
59. http://mashable.com/2011/04/07/watchespn/
60. http://gigaom.com/video/cablevision-ipad-app/
61. http://news.cnet.com/8301-1023_3-20090921-93/viacom-and-cablevi sion-settle-ipad-app-spat/
62. http://www.engadget.com/2011/03/14/time-warner-cables-ipad-app -will-be-the-first-with-live-tv-stre/

63. http://www.slingmedia.com/go/about
64. http://www.lostremote.com/2011/11/14/slingbox-coming-to-facebook
    -soon/
65. http://online.wsj.com/article/SB100014240531119039999045764704 3
    0699007532.html
66. http://gigaom.com/video/fox-piracy/
67. http://techland.time.com/2011/08/24/shocker-piracy-rises-after-fox
    -delays-hulu-shows/
68. http://www.broadcastingcable.com/article/472897-Reports_Deadline
    _for_Hulu_Bids_Extended.php
69. http://blog.hulu.com/2011/10/13/hulu-equity-owners-announce-deci
    sion-to-terminate-the-hulu-sale-process/
70. http://blog.hulu.com/2011/09/22/hulu-now-available-on-facebook/
71. http://blog.nielsen.com/nielsenwire/online_mobile/americans-watch
    ing-more-tv-than-ever/
72. http://assets.huluim.com/downloads/hulu_ad_specs.pdf
73. http://www.adweek.com/news/technology/hulus-ad-selector-could
    -set-web-video-pace-101553
74. http://blog.hulu.com/2011/10/03/the-power-of-choice-in-advertising/

Chapter 9   Connected TVs

1. http://www.cedmagic.com/history/webtv-mat960-int-w100.html
2. http://articles.latimes.com/1997-04-21/business/fi-50920_1_webtv
   -networks
3. http://www.businessweek.com/1997/12/b3519146.htm
4. http://www.zdnet.com/news/webtv-needs-more-than-snapple-to
   -reach-a-mass-audience/96732
5. http://www.wired.com/techbiz/media/news/1997/04/2987
6. http://www.internetworldstats.com/top20.htm
7. http://www.comscore.com/Press_Events/Press_Releases/2011/7/com
   Score_Releases_June_2011_U.S._Online_Video_Rankings
8. http://www.internetworldstats.com/am/us.htm
9. http://gigaom.com/video/online-video-primetime-tv/
10. http://www.forrester.com/rb/Research/make_connected_tvs_future
    _of_tv/q/id/57662/t/2

11. http://www.emarketer.tv/Article.aspx?R=1008347
12. http://techpp.com/2011/03/27/replacement-cycle-why-tvs-are-becoming-like-computers/
13. http://www.reuters.com/article/2011/07/07/idUS162149+07-Jul-2011+BW20110707
14. http://www.apple.com/pr/library/2007/03/21Apple-TV-Now-Shipping.html
15. http://techcrunch.com/2011/04/20/report-the-new-apple-tv-is-selling-well-analyst-puts-total-sales-just-under-2-million-in-7-months/
16. http://www.youtube.com/watch?v=Z535e0imqzw
17. http://thenextweb.com/apple/2011/08/01/apple-tv-update-streams-all-purchased-tv-and-adds-vimeo-support/
18. http://gigaom.com/video/a-first-look-at-google-tv-some-sites-blocked-some-optimized-2/
19. http://paidcontent.org/article/419-viacom-confirms-blocking-access-to-full-episodes-on-google-tv/
20. http://www.digitaltrends.com/home-theater/google-tv-returns-are-outpacing-sales/
21. http://allthingsd.com/20101224/logitech-delaying-new-googletv-too-report/
22. http://gigaom.com/video/new-google-tv-screenshots/
23. http://mashable.com/2011/05/19/boxee-box-review/
24. http://blog.boxee.tv/2011/08/09/boxee-for-ipad-and-more-goodies/
25. http://connectedtv.yahoo.com/newsroom/newsletter/#1
26. http://thenextweb.com/microsoft/2011/05/31/microsoft-40-of-xbox-usage-is-non-game/
27. http://news.cnet.com/Xbox-360-makes-desert-debut/2100-1043_3-5963915.html
28. http://gigaom.com/video/al-jazeera-roku-online-video/
29. http://blog.boxee.tv/2011/09/13/wsj-live-live-and-on-demand-news-on-boxee/
30. http://www.lostremote.com/2011/06/06/live-tv-youtube-bing-coming-to-xbox-live/
31. http://thenextweb.com/2011/10/05/its-official-verizon-bringing-live-tv-to-the-xbox-360/
32. http://techcrunch.com/2011/10/05/microsoft-doubles-down-on-media-reveals-new-xbox-content-partners/

33. http://techcrunch.com/2010/12/06/espn-only-0-11-percent-of-house holds-have-cut-the-cord-and-these-arent-hipster-households-either/

34. http://www.videonuze.com/blogs/?2011-07-20%2017:35:32/SNL -Kagan-Forecasting-10-of-U-S-Homes-Will-Cut-the-Cord-by-2015/ &id=3149

35. http://www.lostremote.com/2011/05/11/roku-users-cutting-the-cord -in-substantial-numbers/

36. http://bits.blogs.nytimes.com/2011/06/15/netflix-helps-people-cut -cable-cord-report-says/

37. http://screenandstream.com/1328/fox-tv-shows-online/

38. http://www.hhcc.com/blog/2011/06/is-your-cable-box-the-next-con nected-tv-device/

39. http://www.nytimes.com/2011/06/21/business/media/21xbox.html

40. http://adverlab.blogspot.com/2011/06/kinect-to-power-tv-ads-bill boards.html

Chapter 10   Conclusion (for Now)

1. http://bet.mediaroom.com/index.php?s=43&item=916

2. http://techcrunch.com/2011/10/17/usa-taps-yap-tv-for-new-social-tv -app/

3. http://www.allfacebook.com/facebook-connect-yahoo-2011-11

4. http://www.digitaltrends.com/home-theater/sharp-unveils-massive-80 -inch-led-lcd-tv-impressions-and-pics/

5. http://www.sharpusa.com/ForHome/HomeEntertainment/LCDTVs/ LC80LE632U.aspx

6. http://books.google.com/books?id=r9sDAAAAMBAJ&pg=PA321

Index